Scattering Seeds

Scattering Seeds

Cultivating
Church Vitality

Stephen Chapin Garner
with Jerry Thornell

ALBAN

Herndon, Virginia
www.alban.org

The Alban Institute
2121 Cooperative Way, Suite 100
Herndon, VA 20171

Unless otherwise noted, all Scripture quotations are from the New Revised Standard Version of the Bible, copyright © 1989, Division of Christian Education of the National Council of the Churches of Christ in the United States of America, and are used by permission.

Scripture references marked ESV are from The Holy Bible, English Standard Version, copyright © 2001 by Crossway, a publishing ministry of Good News Publishers. All rights reserved. ESV Text Edition: 2007

Cover Design by Tobias Becker, Bird Box Design.

Library of Congress Cataloging-in-Publication Data

Garner, Stephen Chapin, 1969-
  Scattering seeds : cultivating church vitality / Stephen Chapin Garner with Jerry Thornell.
      p. cm.
  Includes bibliographical references (p. 173).
  ISBN 978-1-56699-422-4
  1. Leadership--Religious aspects--Christianity. 2. Christian leadership. 3. Church growth. I. Thornell, Jerry. II. Title.
  BV652.1.G376 2011
  254'.5--dc23
                          2011048952

13   14   15   16   VP   5   4   3   2

For our church family and all its members and friends—
past, present, and future.

Contents

Foreword

I think it was the Danish theologian Kierkegaard who said faith is, "Holding the tension of polarity."

The Christian faith is rich in polarities to be held in tension. A core one is the paradoxical claim that Jesus Christ is "fully human" and "fully God." How can anyone be fully this and fully that? Because its tough to hold these two together, different traditions and preachers tend to come down on one side or the other. They emphasize Christ's humanity or Christ's divinity. But the trick, so to speak, is holding the two together. Looking at a baby born in a manger out back and seeing the Lord of history and eternity. It's like a battery. Without both poles, there's no charge.

This is just one of the polar tensions to be held for Christians. In Luke's Gospel the parable of the good Samaritan provokes us to serve our neighbor in need. It concludes with Jesus's words "Go and do likewise." But look at what Luke has placed next, right after the this parable. The story of Jesus's visit to Martha and Mary. Martha would like a little more "doing" from Mary, who instead sits at the feet of Jesus and listens—a response Jesus commended as "the better" way. But which is it the puzzled reader of Luke 10 might ask? Is it "go and do" or "sit and listen"? Answer: Yes. It's both, and it's holding the tension between action and contemplation, between initiative and receptivity.

Paul argues that we are saved by "faith alone" (by which he means not so much our faith as God's faithful initiative in Christ on our behalf and our trust in that), while James tells us, in no uncertain terms, that "faith without works is dead." Which is it? Faith or works? Well, both.

Recently I worked with a congregation that was polarized around two different types and styles of worship and really around two different understandings of God. For one group worship was informal, for the other formal. For the first it was all about knowing God through other people, while for the second it was the experience of God in a majestic sanctuary. Each had a firm grip on a partial truth. One emphasized God's immanence, God's presence and closeness; the other God's transcendence, God's otherness and distance. I suggested neither was right but both were true. Their direction for a vital future might lie in coming together in worship that honored both aspects of the truth about God.

All of this is a way of introducing the story you are about to read. The United Church of Christ Norwell is a congregation that understands itself as both "liberal" and "evangelical." It is committed to Jesus and to being a fully inclusive community of faith. It is justice-oriented and Christ-centered. Their liberality is not based on liberal political theory, but in the liberality and generosity of Jesus. They welcome children in worship, gays in fellowship, the poor in membership because Jesus himself both welcomed and sought those who were pushed to the margins.

Holding together "liberal" and "evangelical" is brilliant. It is also tough and against-the-grain. We live in times of great anxiety. One very common way that people manage their anxiety is by polarization. It's either this or it's that. It's either "liberal" or "conservative," either red or blue, either left or right, either fully God or fully human? Really?

While anxiety pushes toward polarization throughout our culture and only deepens fear and isolation, faith prompts and lives another way, a third way. "For my thoughts," said the prophet

Isaiah, "are not your thoughts, my ways are not your ways." God does not embrace or bless our tendencies toward polarization, but calls us beyond our boxes and over barriers to follow the living One who has gone before us, even Jesus.

So the story of UCC Norwell is remarkable. It is a church that holds the tension of polarity, a congregation that refuses to choose sides between deep faith and genuine engagement in the world. Moreover, it is a church that is vital and growing in a time when 75 percent of mainline Protestant congregations are characterized by two words, "aging" and "declining."

And yet UCC Norwell is also unremarkable. It has known failures and struggles. It has tried things that work and things that did not work. Often it has been surprised by which was which. It is in many ways an ordinary church in an ordinary American town in an increasingly un-churched part of the country, New England. But, of course, our faith teaches us that the extraordinary is found not apart from but in the midst of the ordinary.

Not only are the majority of mainline Protestant churches in American getting older and smaller, but another worrisome pattern is evident. They ask less of people. Because so many people seem busy and stressed and pulled in multiple directions, many churches have lowered the bar. They have accommodated and adjusted themselves to fragmented lives in a culture where convenience is one of our gods. UCC Norwell knows this pressure, but they have chosen a different response. They have dared to ask more, to believe enough in what they are doing, and what God is doing through them, to raise the bar. How they have done this will be instructive to readers of Norwell's story.

One more polarity held in tension here: passion and humility. Sometimes those who are passionate about their work and cause are also arrogant. Sometimes the humble do not seem passionately committed. But our faith and its exemplars from Moses to Jesus, from Mary to Paul, are both passionate and humble. So as Chapin Garner and Jerry Thornell tell the Norwell story, you will hear passion and humility held together. Norwell is a church that is passionate about God in Christ and the good news of the gospel. And yet the story is told with humility, with wonder at what God has done and is doing, with a recognition of how much they have to learn and to grow. It's the right combination and I know you will profit from both its passion and its humility.

Anthony B. Robinson
Author of Changing the Conversation: A Third Way for Congregations *and* Transforming Congregational Culture

Preface

How can the world possibly need another book on church vitality and growth? Given all that has been written on the subject and the thorough chronicling of recent innovations in Christian ministry, what more is to be said and read? And perhaps, more pointedly, who are we, as authors, to assume we can add a note to what has already been a fairly exhaustive conversation? In truth, we are not entirely sure; however, we continue to field numerous requests from congregations in our region for information about how our church, the United Church of Christ in Norwell, Massachusetts, thrives in a climate that is often indifferent and at times even hostile to the church of Jesus Christ. This volume is an attempt to respond to the interest our church has generated over the past decade. It is a story told primarily through the experience of a pastor, with inset reflections from lay members of the UCC Norwell community.

As we begin, it is important to be clear about what we are and what we are not. We are not a megachurch. We are not even a particularly well-polished church. We have experienced our fair share of failures in times past and present. We have spent countless hours on strategic plans only to discover God chuckling away, taking us in entirely unexpected directions. We are a church that, according to a 2009 Trinity College study, makes its home in the least religious region of the country.[1] Our communal life is cultivated in the rocky spiritual soil of New England. We seek Christian vitality in an environment that places more emphasis on children's athletics, vacation planning, and career advancement than it does on matters of faith. We labor in a land where part-time Christianity is the norm for even the most dedicated church members. And yet, over the last decade, we have witnessed remarkable growth in our church. We have watched as our worship attendance, annual giving, and participation in Christian education have nearly doubled. We have joyously received several hundred new members into our faith community. We have seen the revitalization of summer worship in a place where the call of beach and boat tend to be more tantalizing. We have also been blessed to have people travel from nearly two dozen surrounding towns to make our faith community their home. And we have witnessed, with a degree of awe, new ministries taking shape in ways that we could have never envisioned or imagined without the assistance of the Holy Spirit.

Our community is far from perfect, which may be all the more reason to share our story. Like so many communities, we still have peeling paint in our sanctuary, we still long for more resources than we receive on an annual basis, and we still have unresolved issues that remind us that our church is very much of this world. But there is an undeniable spirit of vitality in our community that continues to advance, and this book is our attempt to share what we are learning as we till the soil, plant the seeds, tend the plants, and reap a harvest in what most denominations and church strategists consider the "mission field of New England." We believe that if church vitality can be cultivated in our region of the world, then there is great hope for Christ's church to thrive wherever and however gospel seeds are sown. If it can happen in New England, we believe it can happen anywhere!

What follows in these pages is our best and most honest attempt to share the story of the congregation's innovations in ministry, as well as the continuing challenges we face.

For our part, as the authors of this volume, we are both immensely grateful for the opportunity to work and worship and raise our families at the United Church of Christ in Norwell. Ours is not a perfect community, but it is a community we dearly love. We count our service to this particular family of Christ's people as one of the greatest honors of our lives. We feel privileged to be able to share a bit of our church story, on behalf of our church members, with the wider world.

Most of all, we make this offering in honor of the Lord who has been faithful even when we have not—guiding us, encouraging us, and redirecting us even when we were entirely unaware of that divine guiding presence. Which means, at its core, this book is an offering of praise and thanksgiving to the Lord "who by the power at work within us is able to accomplish abundantly far more than all we can ask or imagine" (Ephesians 3:20).

PART 1

Tilling

CHAPTER 1

Preparing a Pastor

Our congregation's story of how church vitality can take root and grow, in even the most challenging environments, begins with tilling—God's hand in preparing the soil of a congregation and a pastor in a particular place at a particular time. I'll start with my own story of preparation.

CENTRAL PARK PRAYERS

Having graduated from college at the bottom of the recession in the early nineties, I found myself working as a stockbroker at an investment firm in New York City. Recently married, and desiring to attain something of the financial wherewithal that my father had garnered as a banking executive, I began working on Wall Street. Truth be told, entry-level jobs in the financial sector were about the only jobs available to inexperienced college graduates, so I took the only job I could get—at the now defunct Lehman Brothers investment firm. Other than having a father who was well versed in matters of finance, my understanding of the markets was nil. With hard work and much prayer, I passed my licensing exams and set out to make millions of dollars as a successful broker in the Big Apple. However, I soon realized I absolutely hated the work. I found the activity of the markets intriguing, but making cold calls and interrupting people in the middle of their day to offer them financial advice they didn't really need, and I didn't really have to offer, was spiritually enervating. With the stated goal of making five hundred cold calls a day for the firm, my only solace came during my half-hour lunch break, when I would eat and walk around "the Pond" in Central Park praying my heart out. I knew I wasn't where I was supposed to be. I had a sense that God had some specific work for me to do, and my soul was crying out for a more fulfilling vocational life. I was lost and desperately longing to be found.

After toiling in New York City for a couple of years, my wife and I began to dream about other vocational opportunities that might be open to us. One afternoon we took a stroll from our Upper East Side apartment into Central Park. I remember it was a beautiful, sunny spring day, the kind of day when anything seems possible and life itself begins to break out of its hibernative bonds. We sat down on the greening lawn behind the Metropolitan Museum of Art and began to talk about our future together. Neither of us sensed we were headed in the direction the Holy Spirit wanted us to go. But what were we to do? As we began to discuss the possibility of going back to school, my wife asked me what kind of graduate program I might want to enroll in. "I'd go to seminary," I said to my surprise and without missing a beat. I had always assumed I would enter ministry one day. I loved the church. I loved my faith. I loved Jesus Christ. However, as I had told myself for years, I planned on becoming a minister only after I had accomplished something truly important with my life. What that might have been—wealth, notoriety, awards—I now realize pales in comparison to the rich blessings of pastoral ministry in Christ's church. But back in 1994, sitting in Central Park with the woman of faith I loved, having been asked what I wanted to do with the rest of my life, and responding with a desire to enter seminary, I felt as if I had been hit by Moses' staff, which ushered forth life-giving water from one who had been, up to that point, as dumb as a stone.

I realized only in retrospect that my excitement about entering seminary did not yet extend to serving a local church. I suspect I must have known—I would have had to have known—that seminary would be prelude to the parish, but somehow all I could think about was three whole years of being wonderfully sequestered in a faith-filled, awe-inspired bastion of religious learning. My own experience is evidence that it takes only a couple of years on Wall Street to condition a person to buy a fantasy instead of confronting obvious reality.

Entering Seminary

After a death-defying drive to Boston in the 1979 Chevy Impala station wagon my wife and I had bought for $120, our graduate education commenced. Blessedly, my wife was attending law school at Boston University, the same university where I was attending seminary. In fact, our two schools stood adjacent to each other. I could see into the law school from my building, and she could peer into the seminary.

However, on the first day of orientation, I prayed that she wasn't watching. As I entered a reception hall and viewed my fellow students, my jaw dropped. Where were my fraternity brothers, where were the athletes with whom I spent so much of my life, where were the other corporate converts who had left behind the allure of wealth for a life with the Lord? My undergraduate experience was at a college where everyone looked like they had just stepped out of a J. Crew catalog, but in seminary there were people of so many different shapes and sizes, ages and colors that I felt entirely out of place. As I looked at the sea of people with whom I would begin seminary, I admit I was utterly blind to the folks who would become lifelong friends and confidants. I could not see the individuals whose sermons and theological reflections would challenge and inspire me. I could not make out the professors who would mentor me and one day allow me to teach by their side. I stood motionless with questions rushing through my mind, but thankfully no words coming out of my mouth. Are these my people? Is this the school I was so excited to attend? Where were the folks who grew up always eating their lunch at the "cool table" in school? Where were the dynamic and ambitious future pastors who would wind up running our nation's finest Christian establishments? I still feel ashamed of my initial judgments of my classmates that first day of orientation, but it would be dishonest to suggest that I felt confident in my decision to enter seminary at that moment.

Shortly thereafter, my expectations and enthusiasm took a further hit when the dean of the school addressed our incoming class. I will never forget his words. "Each one of you who graduates with your Master of Divinity from this seminary will go on to be the CEO of a failing corporation." As if I needed further confirmation that I had just stumbled into the ranks of a rather disappointing institution! I squirmed in my seat for the remainder of the talk, wondering what I had gotten myself into. Why hadn't I taken the LSAT and gone to law school with my wife? What on earth was I going to learn during the next three years with these people?

DISCOVERING DEATH IN THE CHURCH

It was during my second year in seminary that my passion for pastoral ministry began to take shape. In a sociology of religion course, I was introduced, for the first time, to the rapid decline of the mainline Protestant church. The statistics were shocking. I had always been part of healthy, vital congregations, the kind of churches where you needed to arrive early enough if you wanted a good parking spot and a prime seat in the sanctuary. To see twenty- to thirty-year membership trends within denominations and individual churches that dropped like cliff faces filled me with deep grief. I loved the church, and the church appeared to be dying. Across the board the data reflected a dramatic decline in membership, worship attendance, church school attendance, and annual giving. I learned about denominations laying off employees, cutting core programs, and worrying about a growing number of pastoral vacancies and a dwindling number of younger clergy to fill them. An alarming number of churches were shutting their doors, and many of the defunct yet aesthetically pleasing church buildings in prime urban locations were being converted to high-priced condos. I quickly realized that the sparsely attended churches my wife and I had encountered in New York and Boston represented more than just an urban trend away from church, but a national decline that was more pronounced in certain regions of the country. The Bible Belt and the upper Midwest might still be holding their ground against the forces of secularism, but in regions like the Pacific Northwest and New England, a startling number of churches were in hospice care already receiving a morphine drip. Apparently the dean's warning was on target—churches were clearly failing organizations.

I am well aware of the stages of grief, and as I processed the withering decline of an organization I had loved my whole life long, I experienced many of them. Even with the statistics staring me in the face, initially I didn't want to believe in them. Sure the urban churches I was encountering were struggling, but what city church didn't have its own unique set of challenges? The suburban churches of my youth didn't show any signs of terminal illness. Maybe things were not as bad as they seemed. After denial, I got angry. How could anyone let this happen to the church? Shame on incompetent pastors! Shame on impotent denominational leaders! Shame on a heathen society that so disrespected God! After anger I absolutely felt pain and despair and a twinge of depression. I never liked to lose, and now I appeared to be part of a colossal institutional failure. Was the work of ministry within the church akin to rearranging deck chairs on the *Titanic*? Having signed on to be a pastor, would my vocation be that of a chaplain leading a never-ending funeral procession? All these emotions welled up within me and threatened to overwhelm my sense of call.

However, in relatively short order, my sense of foreboding was replaced with a driving passion that remains with me to this day. I began to feel a burgeoning sense of purpose. If the church was in such desperate shape, if fewer and fewer young people were entering ministry, if the institution that had so nurtured me as a child and as a young adult was in jeopardy, could I imagine a more essential place to be? Having received so much from Christian faith communities over the years, was this not my moment to give back? What could be more satisfying than wading and working through the death of the church in the hope of witnessing a resurrection and resurgence of faith? Oddly, I was hooked. As a second-year seminarian, I suddenly had razor sharp clarity of purpose. Someone had to step up and try to save the church—why not me? I confess, with a fair degree of shame and embarrassment, that it took me a few more years before I realized that the job of "savior" had already been taken. Thankfully, Jesus has proven time and time again that he has remarkable patience with slow learners.

MEGACHURCH MIRACLES

With newly kindled passion for parish ministry and a conviction that I could help save the institution I loved, I began to search for a way to fix what was broken in the church. To my great delight, my searching was met with a flood of information about a new Christian phenomenon: the megachurch. In the mid-nineties, testimonials and network news stories about communities like Willow Creek Community Church in Illinois, Saddleback Community Church in California, and Community Church of Joy in Arizona abounded. There were Harvard Business school case studies about these resurgent institutions that were proving—against all odds—that Jesus's church could be relevant in American society once again. Treat the church like any other high-functioning business, get to know your consumer, and offer a product that is irresistible, and you could see thousands of people join you for worship throughout the week. And the great news was that there was a formula for this kind of success, or at least a framework upon which any congregation could build. Apparently the only thing required was a willingness to change.

Worship needed to change. Organs, hymnals, and bulletins with lengthy and constraining liturgies were out. Praise bands, projected lyrics and images, and seamlessly free-flowing worship were in. Wooden pews and dull sermons were out, comfortable theater seating and interactive messages were in. Worship as a Christian *responsibility* was out, and worship that was a consumer-driven *experience* was in. It all made sense. Why wouldn't the church employ the same effective communication strategies that countless other secular entertainment organizations used on a regular basis? Why should the church be willing to be left behind when amazing technological advances could help propel the message of Jesus Christ into the twenty-first century and beyond?

The church building needed to change. Poor signage, bad coffee, and poorly lit bathrooms were out, while welcome centers, quality café-style coffee, and state-of-the-art lavatories were in. Cramped and poorly laid out floor plans were out, and expansive and easily accessible shopping mall churches were in. Haphazardly maintained church grounds, poorly lined parking spots, and dusty church school rooms were out; perfectly manicured landscapes, up-front visitor parking, air-conditioning, and spotless educational spaces were in. Who could argue with those upgrades? If the church was really God's house, and if we were really God's people, shouldn't the physical plant somehow radiate God's glory and extravagant welcome? If Christians wanted people to enter their community, shouldn't the facility be as welcoming as possible?

Church programming needed to change. One worship service for everyone, education only for children, and board and committee work left for adults was out; generational-specific worship, education for everyone, and extensive paid staff teams were in. The church as a sleepy community all but one day a week was out, and church as a 24/7/365 beehive of activity was in. Annual service projects for saintly members were out and congregationally based ministry placement services for new members were in. Who could resist that kind of excitement and vitality? Why should any church settle for meeting the lowest of expectations when clearly so much more was possible? Why be a CEO of a failing organization when pastors were becoming self-proclaimed bishops of successfully branded religious conglomerates?

As news coverage of this megachurch phenomena grew, as best-selling how-to books were being produced by popular pastors, and with church consultants promising that "this too could be your congregation," I was convinced the dying church that I dearly loved could be saved.

Big Plans to Save the Church

The church could be saved, and I could be a part of making it happen! That was the good news that I grabbed hold of as I prepared to graduate from seminary. I began to dream of making a significant impact on American Christianity by creating the first megachurch in New England. I admit that I never bothered to discover if a church of that size and scope already existed in the region, which, of course, it did. So, I began to outline plans to help build, or rebuild, a Christian community that would become a mega-success. I could envision the perfect location for my church, the ideal theological stance, as well as the glitzy marketing campaign that could launch the entire effort. What a coup it would be to show the world that a dynamic and vital community could take root and grow in religiously chilly New England! I would become that pastor whom other pastors looked to in order to discover the secrets to church growth and vitality. My ministry would be widespread and readily embraced. There were moments when I questioned whether or not my dreams were too grandiose, but I quickly swept away any of those doubts, confident in my own abilities and insights. Was it not possible for there to be another important awakening in the land of the pilgrims and Puritans? It had happened before, it could happen again. Exiting seminary, I was confident that growing a church in New England was a manageable feat and one I would be able to accomplish with relative ease. All I needed was my megachurch construction checklist and a church with significant growth potential that was willing to take a chance on a newly minted pastor just out of seminary.

This is a long way of saying that I left seminary with a whole lot more to learn about parish ministry, leadership in general, and Christianity in particular. Like every seminarian that blusters out of school overly confident that they know everything that is wrong with the church and how to fix it, I just did not know how much I did not know. When I look back on my early hopes and aspirations for myself as a pastor and for the church I would serve, I find myself spiritually cringing and trying to take solace in the fact that I wasn't intentionally trying to do any harm. Thankfully, the Holy Spirit has a way of interceding to protect both naïve pastors and the communities that might suffer under their less than careful leadership.

BACKSEAT APPRENTICESHIP

I put together my resume and set out to find my future megachurch. I believed I knew what I was looking for. I wanted a church in a sizable population center. I wanted a church with a parking lot and some property upon which to expand. I wanted a church where people were prepared and excited for change. Ideally, the congregation would have a bit of an endowment that could be used to fund initiatives until growth provided enough income to propel new ministries. And, of course, I wanted to be in charge so that I could make sure everything went according to plan. I had my checklist in mind; I just needed to settle on the right location for its implementation.

However, when it comes to matters and processes of faith, things seldom work out according to plan. To my surprise, my call came not from a congregation wanting to reshape the way ministry is done in New England but from Wellesley Congregational Church in Massachusetts, a well-established church that had little need for my master plans for reshaping the life of Christian community. I was employed as the fourth pastor of a four-pastor church. I was hired to be the associate pastor for youth ministry, a position typically reserved for energetic pastors who were more qualified to play dodge ball with teenagers than to be taken seriously as an agent of change within well-established church leadership. As I began my career in parish ministry, I found myself taking a backseat to an impressive ministerial team. A backseat was the last thing I wanted, but it turned out to be exactly what I needed. Every day, I had the opportunity to watch three extremely talented and faithful pastors engage in ministry, and I realized that the Holy Spirit had graciously allowed me an extended opportunity to learn. In a very real way, seminary had not ended for me; rather, as an associate pastor at a wonderfully healthy church, my ministerial training had just begun. In relatively short order, I became aware of the fact that pressing my own agenda was far less important than shutting my mouth, opening my eyes and ears, and watching for where the Holy Spirit was already at work. I began to doubt that my mega-agenda had much merit at all. In fact, I was slowly coming to terms with the very real possibility that a church's agenda must be the Lord's, and not the pastor's, if a congregation is to head in the right direction.

For three years I watched, listened, and learned in my role as a youth minister. I was witness to well-laid plans that fell apart entirely, as well as miracles of transformation that seemed to occur well beyond my ability to influence. I developed a suspicion that a pastor did not have to drive a congregation in a particular direction to be successful, but rather a pastor simply had to find ways to nudge open windows and doors and other passageways so that the Spirit had an entry point into people lives. A pastor should not be the primary mover but rather a catalyst for the movement of the Spirit within Christian community. My job was not to implement specific initiatives on a church growth checklist, but to yield to the Spirit so that Jesus might lead. I began to wonder, was church growth about a strategic implementation of a new vision for ministry, or was church growth the result of faithful tending to seeds that were already sown in congregational soil? Maybe the job of a pastor wasn't to do anything different, but to be something different. The pastor wasn't called to be a CEO of anything. The call to ministry wasn't a call to take charge. Success couldn't be forced any more than shouting at a seed would make it germinate and grow. What if my job was about waiting, watching, and witnessing to the work of God in the world, while tending to the growth that only God could provide? Imagine that!

Three years out of seminary, I found I was far less certain about the purpose and practice of ministry, which might just have been a sign that I was perhaps ready for more responsibility. Unbeknownst to me, while I was struggling to understand how to be a pastor, there was a church that was struggling to become a family again.

Questions for Reflection

1. What evidence of mainline congregational decline have you experienced or witnessed firsthand as a pastor or congregation member? What exceptions to mainline

congregational decline have you experienced or witnessed
in your congregation?

2. As lay leader or pastor, think about your passion for ministry and the desire to "save the church." How do those mo-
   tivations play out in your life as a congregational leader?
   How have they been effective? How have they gotten in the
   way of what God is doing?

3. If you are an ordained leader, how have your passion and
   expectations for ministry changed over time, from your
   first days out of seminary to today?

4. Think of a time when God, it seemed, interrupted your
   agenda for the congregation you serve. What happened?

5. For your congregation now, is "church growth about a strategic implementation of a new vision for ministry," or is
   it "the result of faithful tending to seeds that were already
   sown in congregational soil"?

CHAPTER 2

Preparing a Congregation

As I was reexamining my ideas about the pastor's role in church growth and plotting a course for my next call, a church located not far from me was also reexamining its approach to ministry. My plans took some unexpected twists and turns, showing me that the Holy Spirit was alive and well—and in charge of pastoral relocation.

THE SUGAR-SHACK CHURCH

After a fairly swift and whirlwind-like job search, my wife and I believed we had found the church we were called to. It was a large multistaff church in a very affluent suburb of Boston, with a great school system and wonderful recreational activities. The church was a quintessentially gorgeous church-on-the-green, with its accompanying historic parsonage. It was everything we could have hoped and dreamed for ourselves. As we entered the final stages of our negotiation with what we believed would be our new church home, I began to cancel other interviews that I had scheduled with additional churches. Both my wife and I believed our search was over. And then one afternoon, I received an unexpected package from a church I hadn't even applied to. Inside were materials that told the story of a relatively young, vibrant, midsized church in a town I had never heard of on the South Shore of Massachusetts. Having already settled on the church I planned to serve, I remember nearly discarding the materials until a pencil sketch of the physical plant caught my eye. It was an unusual looking building that didn't fully resemble a church. I would later learn that it had been designed to evoke the image of a New England sugarshack. The curious exterior prompted me to take a longer look at what was going on within the community. The profile highlighted a unique theological stance, expansive mission engagements, an unusual commitment to the ministry of the laity in their workplaces, and an undeniable entrepreneurial spirit. The profile of the church did not hide the painful history and division that had been experienced by the membership. I was impressed by both the honesty and the innovation of the congregation. The church also sat on nearly seventeen acres of land with an enormous parking lot that few churches in New England could claim to have. Even though I believed my search was complete, my interest was piqued. Knowing that my mind was made up, I didn't want to mislead this church on the South Shore, but I couldn't suppress the urge to find out a bit more about this sugar-shack church. After consulting my wife, I decided to go on one last interview.

LIFE AT UCC NORWELL

The United Church of Christ in Norwell was still a relatively young church in our denomination, it was not even forty years old and yet it had already experienced the tremendous highs and the heart-wrenching lows of our most historic congregations. For its first two decades of life, UCC Norwell had been a model of creative and dynamic ministry. The community grew at a

This drawing of the United Church of Christ, Norwell, Massachusetts, was done by Joel H. Clemons, Hanson, Massachusetts.

remarkable pace, drawing people from all over the South Shore. It had a unique blend of liberal and evangelical theology that allowed the community to passionately claim Jesus Christ as central to its gathered life, while being a remarkably inclusive community. They were a church that was committed to prayer and to the authority of Scripture. It had a history of burgeoning youth groups and impressive mission and outreach initiatives. The community had seemed to succeed at every ministry they engaged in, and, as a result, the church developed a bit of a swagger. UCC Norwell felt special, as if anything it wanted to accomplish was within its grasp. And then, in the late 1980s and early 1990s, the members of UCC Norwell found themselves in a congregation-splitting leadership transition. During a very unsettled and unsettling time of interim, the community began to fracture. A community that was accustomed to success and growth suddenly had to come to terms with brokenness and failure. They sustained significant membership and financial losses. Members who had once held hands in prayer together found they didn't want to speak to one another when they ran into each other at the supermarket. It was an awful mess—a story familiar to almost every church at one time or another.

However, those who chose to endure and remain in the community slowly began the hard work of healing. Thanks to a decade of thoughtful and careful pastoral leadership, and the perseverance of faithful lay leaders, the painful wrangling of the past crisis was worked through. Slowly, as trust began to return, difficult topics could again be addressed without congregation-wide contention. In fact, during one interim period, the United Church of Christ in Norwell engaged in a very healthy conversation about whether or not to welcome and affirm people who are gay, lesbian, bisexual, or transgendered into the life of the church. In what could have been a very divisive conversation, the members of UCC Norwell engaged one another with great love and respect, proving that difficult issues didn't have to be a prelude to knock-down-drag-out church fights. Disagreements didn't have to end in family estrangement. The trials of the cross could lead to real resurrection.

By the spring of 2000, UCC Norwell had emerged as a much humbler community. It was a community that was prepared for a fresh start. It was a community that was ready to set aside its own agenda—to the best of its ability—in order to follow the Spirit's leading. To look back on it now, it was as if the Holy Spirit had been preparing a young church and a young pastor for one another. They just needed the opportunity to meet.

DATING AND FALLING IN LOVE

Without much expectation or interest, I entered into conversation with the members of the search committee at the United Church of Christ Norwell. One interview became two, and then a tour of

the community with my wife, a dinner with the search committee, and an offer of employment. We had only just begun dating,
but already we were falling in love. I knew that a search committee, by design, is made up of the best the community has to offer.
They are the chosen ambassadors of the church, selected because
they are capable, engaging, and committed to the future of their
institution. They may even care about the faith they are working to
preserve. I was immediately impressed by the group I met with in
Norwell. They were friendly, bright, and thoughtful, but more than
that, they were genuinely prayerful. Every pastor knows that at the
end of an interview he or she will be asked to close the gathering
with a prayer. I was struck by the fact that the search committee
that I was coming to love, never asked me to pray. They were the
ones who prayed for me, for our time together, and for the Spirit
to offer us all the direction we needed. While I was intrigued by
many aspects of the community's life, it was the prayers offered in
our time together that made me realize that Norwell was the place
I wanted to be. There may have been some ugly church fights in
the past. The physical structure of the church might have been a
bit odd and unconventional. The town itself might have been difficult to locate on a map. But through their prayers, I sensed that
something special had taken place in Norwell, and I had a growing
belief that something remarkable could happen if we entered into
ministry together. With some reluctance, my wife and I decided it
was time to call the gorgeous church-on-the-green and let them
know that the Spirit was taking us to another community. In what
seemed like little more than a matter of days, we got officially engaged and a few months later we had our marriage ceremony that
took the form of a service of installation. It all happened so fast,
and yet it seemed so right. Inevitably, the speed with which we had
decided to get hitched was followed by a time of adjustment that
had all of us wondering what we had gotten ourselves into.

WAKING UP IN THE MIDDLE OF NOWHERE

What I remember most about our first days in Norwell were my wife's tears. We hadn't really gotten a thorough tour of the area, so we didn't even know where the nearest grocery store was. In fact, we didn't know where much of anything was. My wife's commute to her Boston law firm had grown in duration and complexity. We had been told how wonderful it was to live not far from the ocean, though for the life of us we could not find any nonresident parking at the beach. And in a thoughtful effort to give us some space, church members had been careful not to flood us with calls and visits, which left us feeling a bit lonely. Hence the tears and the growing sense of frustration. For my part, I began to wrestle with the reality of living in a town that most people in Massachusetts had never heard of before. Norwell was one of the smallest bedroom communities of Boston—so small that it didn't have its own dot on many Massachusetts maps. It was as if we had gone to sleep and then had woken up in the middle of nowhere. Slowly but surely, I felt the creeping presence of panic. How were people going to find us? How were we going to grow? Had I made a colossal misstep in my career by settling in uncharted and rather unremarkable hinterlands? Of course, the real concerns were buried far beneath the surface in a place I wasn't ready to admit existed. Since I wasn't ready to deal with them in the daylight, the deeply rooted concerns quickly began to haunt me well into the night, making sleep fitful at best. Now that I was on the job, I began to worry that I wasn't up for the challenge. Where had the bravado of my seminary years gone? Had my time in the backseat of the Wellesley Congregational Church served to cultivate a fear of getting on the road myself? Did I have the ability to make good on the hopes the Norwell community had for their new pastor? My concerns stemmed from the fact that even before I had arrived, the United

Church of Christ in Norwell had begun to move, and I needed to find a way to quickly jump on board.

✌ ✌

The seeds of change for UCC Norwell were sown at the leadership retreat in October of 1997 (with the birth of what was to become Project 2000) and reached maturity in 2001 with a new leadership structure in place. While these dates benchmark the period of transformation, change is constant, and the church has continued to evolve in a most healthy way since that time.

Several catalytic events occurred during this period that contributed to the success of the transformation. In 1998, the nominating committee was faced with the challenge of replacing 43% of the members of the existing church boards. In our changing society, where two wage earners were now being needed and were also raising a family, it was becoming very difficult to find people who would commit to three years of board service. This proved to be a catalyst for more self-selected volunteering. In 1999, the church voted to reduce its expenses by approximately 10% in order to live within its means. This was implemented by the elimination of an ordained staff person, certainly a catalyst for needing ministry from the laity. In 2000 the congregation voted to become "open and affirming" and that became a catalyst for a statement of our core values. Finally, the calling of Reverend Garner, a young pastor, who endorsed the church's direction, was a catalyst for pulpit leadership and encouragement.

Back in October 1997, the church council had hosted a leadership retreat based on a two year study effort of, what was then, the Ministry in Daily Life committee. Two task forces evolved from that meeting. One was to focus on the organizational structure and leadership model of the church. The other was to study how to better utilize the gifts and talents of the congregation. A third action item was a request of the Christian Education board to review the timing of church school and adult education relative to Sunday worship. Collectively, this undertaking became known as Project 2000.

We were entering into a time of new lay involvement with pastoral help, all dedicated to the fulfillment of our new mission statement. It is amazing how God shows us the way to accomplish His work with our lives.

Joe Aten, founder and president of Fibertec
and former moderator at UCC Norwell

꙳ ꙳

A CHURCH ON THE MOVE

Whatever ministerial lulls the church had experienced during its years of conflict, UCC Norwell had begun to move—and rapidly! As they peered into the twenty-first century, the church decided it was time to reenvision its future. Even though they had suffered and struggled their way through the preceding decade, they still believed their best years were ahead of them. They engaged in a process they called Project 2000, which they hoped would help them restructure their administrative life as a community so they could break free from the encumbering systems of the past. They recognized that they had significant commitment and participation in mission trips and outreach ministries, while at the same time they struggled to recruit enough people to fill the annual slate of nominees for their numerous board and committees. They longed for a stronger sense of fellowship, but understood that significant tasks needed to be accomplished if the church was to maintain its communal integrity. They suspected that the traditional church structure that organized their community was no longer working, but they were not entirely sure of what organizing principles might be more effective. After a couple of years of thoughtful discussion and discernment, the Project 2000 team began to float the idea that the church should jettison its overburdened "board and committee" structure and move to a more nimble "ministry team" model.

While the transition from boards and committees into ministry teams will be the focus of another chapter, it is important to note that the church was gearing up for a significant change in their gathered life just as I was beginning my service as their new pastor. This presented me with the pressing need to understand, affirm, and begin to implement the new model, while at the same time trying not to look as if I were the primary agent of change within the church. I felt as though I was trying to jump on a moving train. As is the case with much church visioning, the members of the task force were out ahead of much of the congregation, many of whom naturally assumed that the new pastor was the impetus behind all the new structural proposals. During my first month on the job, I realized that UCC Norwell wasn't a sleepy church waiting for their new pastor to give them direction; they were a community going full steam ahead, and I found myself rushing to try to catch up. I had to get a handle on what this community was trying to become, even before I had a chance to learn much about who they had been in the years preceding my arrival.

꒷ ꒦

I remember sitting at a meeting in a living room one evening in 2001 talking about replacing the traditional church structure of nominated committees with ministry teams—to which people would feel called based on their passions. Also on the table were groundbreaking ideas about different ways to staff our church, including calling our minister a "teaching pastor." Wow. In thinking later about this evening and countless others like it over the life of what we called "Project 2000," I would think about another group of people—including my parents—who gathered in another living room some 40 years earlier to talk about starting a new Congregational church in Norwell. That church would be UCC Norwell.

Among us that night in 2001 was our new young pastor, Chapin Garner. I remember him smiling and being supportive, but letting members in the room take the lead. I remember many of the faces around the room, all dear to me. In his letter in the January 2001 annual report, just six months into his ministry with us, Chapin wrote about his belief that the Holy Spirit "may choose to speak through the most unexpected member of the church, and often does." He continued, ". . . next time that voice might be yours, or it might be the person seated next to you—that is why our primary job is to listen." Having been a part of this congregation of folks since I was in second grade, I knew Chapin was right. I'd seen it happen on more than one occasion, in living rooms just like the one in which we sat that night. Ordinary people saying and doing extraordinary things—yet to me it seemed like something of a way of life. It never occurred to me not to trust my church family—or not to trust that we'd be led to be bold and try new things.

We'd come a long way as a church to that night in 2001. My parents were part of the congregation that called another remarkable young pastor named David Norling to UCC Norwell back in 1969. When Dave moved on nearly 20 years later, he left a vacuum that was filled, slowly and sometimes nearly imperceptibly, with various forms of dysfunction and disarray. When the situation evolved into crisis, our beloved church suffered deep division and pain.

In the years before Chapin joined us in 2000, the members of UCC Norwell had accompanied one another back to relative health as a church, thanks to a few years of good pastoral leadership and many, many loving, patient, and committed members. But we were changed, especially in one fundamental way. We had a new, hard-won understanding of church as led by Jesus Christ—not by any single person—staffed along the way by talented pastors, and filled with dedicated members. The fact that we were healthy enough to call an exceptionally gifted pastor like Chapin seemed to be evidence of our newfound maturity. Chapin encouraged our new understanding of Christ as head of the church, and that knowledge gave us all the freedom to thrive, grow, and take some risks.

Betsy Baldwin Brink, Assistant Director, MBA communications and marketing, Harvard Business School, and daughter of UCC Norwell charter members

꒳ ꒳

CATALYST FOR CHANGE

I found all the changes exciting and I was glad to be at a church that was on the move; however, I found it difficult to come to terms with the perception that I was the one spear heading all the adjustments to the church. I was only thirty years old, and members of the community who had been the driving force behind the creation of the church began to wonder why such a young pastor felt encouraged to enact significant changes from the moment he came to the church. There were people who became upset, there were people who left the church in a huff, and a number of angry letters found their way to my desk.

The first few months at UCC Norwell were overwhelming; I was trying to hop on the train without getting caught from behind by people who believed I might be ruining the church. It was an awkward position to be in. I wasn't responsible for the innovation and exciting vision work that was being done, nor was I responsible for the discomfort that began to result from the changes that were being implemented. I resolved to simply try to find ways to love the people while not taking too seriously any criticism that was directed my way. However I planned to manage my pastoral life, I was acutely aware that I was not in control. My lack of control may have been the most important and lasting realization of those first days of ministry at UCC Norwell. As pastor, I was not going to be in control, I was not going to be taking the lead, I was not going to be the one initiating changes within our community. In fact, I was told rather directly by one of the moderators of the church that if I exercised too much influence over the work the church was doing, I might actually disempower the very people we were hoping to more thoroughly engage in ministry.

MINISTRY OF THE LAITY

Capable pastors do have a way of disempowering people. Laity will almost always defer to competent pastoral leadership. A strong pastoral staff could inadvertently produce a weak church. I didn't like the message, though I understood the truth of it. One of the first lessons I learned from the members of UCC Norwell was that they were the ministers. That was not merely a slogan on the front cover of the Sunday bulletin; it was etched in the hearts and minds of almost all of the lay leaders of the church. The people were the ministers; the pastors were simply there to tend to the people. It was impressed on me that I needed to understand my place. For many of the members of the church, the painful leadership transition of the previous decade was, in part, due to the church's reliance on extremely gifted pastoral leadership. The church had grown into a pastor-centered church, and when the pastor left, the church family began to fracture. The community did not want to repeat those mistakes, and so they were careful to make sure I knew that my place was beside them, not in front of them. It was a model of ministry that was foreign to me, but I was willing to try to make it work.

I was supposed to lead from the middle, as a shepherd in their midst, not as a visionary planting a flag out ahead of them while encouraging them to "charge!" I was not to be a CEO, and I was not going to be able to take much credit for the failing or succeeding of the community I was serving. Frankly, I was not prepared for this new kind of ministry, which only enhanced my sense of being out of control. As I look back, I realize that none of us were really in control. We didn't really know what we were doing. We were fooling ourselves if we thought that reorganizing the structural life of our church would turn out to be our salvation. If we did anything right as we sought a new vision for our life together more than a decade ago, it was the prayer, study, and communal discernment we engaged in. Through this, we were unwittingly opening ourselves up to the movement of the Holy Spirit. We unknowingly opened the door and the Holy Spirit entered, and from that moment on, control was in someone else's hands. Only in hindsight did I come to realize that God was doing something remarkable at Norwell and we were all just along for the ride. The more I got to know my new congregation, I clearly recognized that this was not the first time the Holy Spirit had had its way with this gathering of people.

LEARNING THE HISTORY

In those frenetic early days, I gathered as much history as I could on the fly. I met with church members during the day to listen to their stories of the joys and trials of the church, while meeting at night with different task forces assigned to remodel different aspects of the community's life. My days were given over to learning about the past, and my nights were full of visions for the future. It was an exciting yet exhausting juxtaposition that should have clued me into an important aspect of the character of the community. From its very beginnings, UCC Norwell had been graciously at the mercy of the Holy Spirit—a Spirit that tends to blow where it chooses and tends to resist all attempts to control it.

Decades before Project 2000, and well before a church building was erected in a vacant pasture on a busy stretch of Norwell's
main street, a small gathering of people met in a living room on
that same street to talk about starting a new church. The year was
1965, and the motivating intention was rather selfish, if the truth
is to be told. Armed with what they believed were their best inten-
tions, a dozen or so residents of Norwell got together over coffee and blueberry muffins to talk about the possibility of having
their very own Congregational church in town. They were tired
of going to church in neighboring towns. They wanted their own
church, filled with people from their own neighborhoods, with
children from their own school system. If every single town in
Massachusetts could have its own Congregational church, why
couldn't they have one too?

Even in the moments of its inception, the unique and unpredictable nature of God's Holy Spirit could be seen at work. Over
forty-five years ago, a group of people began to prayerfully make
plans for a new town church. They planted a church that was intended to meet the exclusive needs of their local community, and
yet within a few years the church began to draw people from all
over the South Shore of Massachusetts. To this day, we have more
church members from out of town than we do from the town of
Norwell itself. The people felt called to start a new local church,
and the Holy Spirit decided to use the opportunity to birth a re-
gional community of faith.

Time and time again that has been the story of the United
Church of Christ in Norwell. We have tried on numerous occasions to be strategic about our planning only to have the Holy
Spirit take us in entirely unexpected directions. The story of our
little sugar-shack church is one of people opening themselves up
to the Holy Spirit, and then attempting to follow the leading of the
Spirit to the best of their ability. It is a story of how missteps can
lead to miracles when a community releases its need to be in control all the time. This means our story is a good news story that can

be experienced by any community willing to risk a little chaos in pursuit of the gospel. We have discovered that when we are finally willing, the Spirit is more than able!

Questions for Reflection

1. Where have you been aware the Holy Spirit's guidance in your journey in ministry, both personally and congregationally?

2. Are you "willing to risk a little chaos in pursuit of the gospel"? That is, if the ministry task is to open yourself to the Holy Spirit's leading, and then attempt to follow, what in this approach makes you feel uncomfortable? What seems risky? What in this approach feels comfortable, reassuring, or familiar? When have you experienced "missteps lead to miracles"?

3. If the vision for mission and ministry in your congregation primarily comes from the pastor, the board, or other lay leaders, think of a time when the impetus for a new ministry arose in an unexpected way. What happened? How did it go?

4. What does, or might, the pastor leading from the middle look like in your congregation? Where is that already happening? Where it's not happening, imagine, in detail, the changes that would need to be made for it to happen and how the scenario might begin to unfold in a way that's healthy and respectful.

PART 2

Scattering Seeds

CHAPTER 3

Soil, Climate, and the Mystery of Growth

As we attempted to follow the Spirit's lead in the ministry of UCC Norwell, our own carefully formulated plans often didn't have the results we intended. In spite of ourselves, the congregation experienced miracles, surprises, and growth in numbers. I no longer possessed my seminary-inspired ambition to pursue growth for growth's sake, but I was still very intrigued by how growth can take hold in a community of faith. What elements need to be in place to ignite church growth? Are there certain keys to cultivating vibrant communal life? Perhaps there is not a specific checklist or formula for growth, but are there any guidelines that a pastor could count on?

A QUESTION OF GROWTH

Cultivating a lively community of faith is not rocket science or brain surgery. I am now well aware that people attend church for some very basic reasons. People go to church to hear a consistent word—sermons are as essential to the life of a church today as they have ever been. People go to church because they love the music—faith has been powerfully conveyed through song and stanza for generations. People go to church because their children are well taken care of—they receive assistance passing on the Christian tradition within their families. Dynamic sermons, music, and children's programming can certainly propel growth. With only one of these components in place, a community can experience increase. In truth, it would be hard to avoid growth if a community had all three working together.

But what propels exponential growth? What allows a church to grow out of a staid and stable program-based model of ministry into a transformative, life-altering community of believers? How does new and innovative ministry take hold within a community whose historical strength has been its resistance to change and its ability to endure against all odds? I did not know, but after only a couple of years at UCC Norwell I began to witness a pattern of growth that was as surprising as it was unsettling. We seemed to be growing in spite of ourselves, and in the most unplanned of ways . . . and I suspect that deep down I was still hoping for an approach to church growth that involved following a list of well-defined steps toward success.

Plans Going Wonderfully Awry

Over the last decade, we at UCC Norwell have engaged in numerous visioning processes, and none of them have turned out the way we had imagined they would. We would pull together a task force to address some issue of concern, meetings would be held for weeks on end, recommendations would be generated and presented to the church, resolutions would be voted on, and new programs and structures would be put into place, only to discover that we missed the mark and growth was occurring in an entirely different location than that which we had expected.

One of the earliest examples of this frustratingly wonderful pattern occurred within the first couple of years we spent working together. I had been working with the Alban Institute in an effort to gain clarity about the dearth of young clergy in mainline Protestant denominations. After gathering statistics from across the country, we confirmed that the lack of young people entering ministry in mainline denominations threatened the long-term health and viability of our brand of church. The math was as simple as it was disheartening. The trickle of young clergy entering pastoral ministry could not meet the great wave of ministerial retirements that could be anticipated on the horizon. Even with an increased number of second-career pastors, the impending pastoral vacancies were going to dwarf the pool of available applicants.

Armed with this irrefutable evidence of the demise the church I loved, I convinced UCC Norwell that we needed to begin to prepare ourselves to be a church without clergy. Even though I believed we were still ahead of the curve by a few years, we needed to get the church ready for the impending clergy crisis. We began by convening a task force to examine how we could more fully establish ourselves as a lay-led congregation. The result of an extensive period of discernment was to establish a new model for pastoral ministry that deemphasized the role of ordained clergy. No longer was the program life of the church going to be created and driven by professional religious leaders. If a program was going to be implemented in the life of our church, it needed to be generated by the efforts and initiative of church members. Pastors were no longer to engage in ministry unless they were helping to train lay members for the ministerial tasks before them.

We created a Teaching Pastorate model for ministry that stressed preparing the laity to take on the work of the church. The idea was expansive. Fully implemented, the people of the church would do the pastoral care, the teaching of children and adults, the preaching and worship leadership, and the visioning of the future. We didn't plan to make immediate and radical adjustments, but we knew we needed to slowly shift aspects of pastoral ministry to the laity. For example, the members of the church wanted a comprehensive adult education program that the church had never really established before. Our pastoral staff could have simply jumped in and started offering classes. However, with the desire to have the laity lead, we created an adult Christian education ministry team that, with a modest amount of pastoral support, would design, promote, and teach the educational offerings for our adults. Within a relatively short period, we not only increased the number of lay members in leadership roles, but we also took a gigantic leap forward in the number of adult educational offerings we provided for the congregation. The energy the new group possessed was impressive, and it was clear they not only appreciated how they had been empowered to engage in ministry, but they also stepped up and did amazing work—work many trained pastors would not be capable of achieving.

Efforts like this were made with the intention of crafting a community that could one day move forward without having the need of professional clergy. It was a compelling idea. We were already seeing signs that strong lay leadership could replace pastoral leadership in certain instances. We seemed to be on our way to being a church that could thrive without clergy. That had been the plan and we were prepared to make an attempt to implement it. However, that was when the Holy Spirit began to upend our plans.

Soon thereafter, church members began making appointments with me to talk about the possibility of entering seminary. One after another, church members were sensing a call to pastoral ministry. In a period of four years we sent seven church members to seminary. We had set out to create a model for ministry that would allow the church to survive without clergy, and we unwittingly created a model of ministry that prompted people to choose to pursue pastoral ministry as a career. We had a plan, we had a goal, we had an end result in mind, and our efforts had an effect that we never intended. In an attempt to create a clergy-free church, we wound up creating clergy that are now serving local churches in our area.

So many times in UCC Norwell's ministry together we have done what we believed to be faithful discernment—we set our sights on a goal, we began our work, only to have the Holy Spirit produce growth in an entirely different direction than we intended. It has happened with such frequency that I have begun to think that any attempt to be strategic in the life of the church is fraught with peril. And yet, perhaps the effort to grow, no matter how misguided, uniquely opens us up to the possibility and potential of the Holy Spirit. When we give the Spirit an opening to work in our churches, that is when growth takes root even in the most unexpected of ways. To this day, I am amazed at how getting it wrong has turned out to be just right.

Locally Defined Character and Flavor

It is quite disconcerting to experience growth but not fully understand what produced it. How can you duplicate results in the future if you do not grasp what is happening in the present? And if our lack of knowledge and understanding was not enough to unsettle us, the fact that we had put forth our best efforts and pursued a vision that was not realized was truly confusing. What was happening? Why couldn't we plan for growth when other organizations seemed to be doing so with exacting precision? I know there are effective formulas for growth, because those formulas can be seen in big-box stores and big-box churches that proliferate all over the country. Chain restaurants and chain churches demonstrate that if you market the right concept in just the right way, success is there to be had. If you build it—and you build it correctly—people will come. So why were we experiencing exciting growth but never in the areas we intended?

I have come to believe that while there are impressive and effective models for growth and expansion that can be witnessed in multinational corporations as well as multiple-campus churches, there is also a very real and powerful local growth movement afoot. There are mom and pop restaurants whose customers swear they serve the best food in the world, there are local grocers whose specialty products can't be found anywhere else, and there are community banks that thrive because they tend to the particular needs of the towns they serve. While it is comforting that big-box stores all look alike—you know exactly in which aisle dishwasher detergent can be found and you can locate the electronics department with your eyes closed—it is intriguing to find the unexpected in a little shop you might have missed if you were looking the wrong way as you drove down the street. Case in point is the incredibly popular local farm that still delivers milk in glass bottles to the suburban communities south of Boston. Everyone in our area loves Hornstra Farms. You can find their small cooler boxes next to doorways throughout our region. They deliver locally produced items that range from eggs to pizza, heavy cream to ice cream, chicken pot pies to cinnamon swirl bread. The service isn't cheap, and the operation has become more polished over the years, but it is a uniquely local phenomenon that will not be overtaken by the big-chain grocery store's delivery service. Local business has become big business in the communities they serve.

I don't want to dismiss what can be learned from the impressive megachurches in our country. When we discount their accomplishments and find fault with their methods, it is often because we are jealous we cannot replicate their results. However, not all towns want a gargantuan faith community to serve their religious needs, just as well-known big-box stores aren't isn't always welcome in every community in which they try to establish themselves. There is still reason to believe that the local church is supposed to be undeniably *local* in its character and make up. You never know who will walk through the doors of the local church and make a lasting impact. And a community's character will directly reflect the unique personalities of the individuals that make it up. No two local churches will look the same. No two local churches will grow the same. No two local churches will have exactly the same mission and ministry. And surprise, surprise; that reality seems to suit the Holy Spirit just fine!

A THEOLOGY OF GROWTH

If growth and vitality in faith communities are not always products of careful planning or effective strategizing, how can they be explained? How does local, unique, and surprising growth take root? I wondered, was there a theology for growth and vitality that could explain what we were witnessing in Norwell, Massachusetts? As is my custom, I turned to the Bible for guidance. I knew that Jesus's ministry wasn't exactly strategic in nature. Paul certainly had a vision for his travels, but circumstance often forced him to change course. The miracle of Pentecost wasn't planned for as far as I could tell, and yet it happened all the same. What did the Bible have to say about growth? Two very familiar parables leapt off the page toward my questioning mind.

> Listen! A sower went out to sow. And as he sowed, some seed fell on the path, and the birds came and ate it up. Other seed fell on rocky ground, where it did not have much soil, and it sprang up quickly, since it had no depth of soil. And when the sun rose, it was scorched; and since it had no root, it withered away. Other seed fell among thorns, and the thorns grew up and choked it, and it yielded no grain. Other seed fell into good soil and brought forth grain, growing up and increasing and yielding thirty and sixty and a hundredfold.
>
> Mark 4:3–8

> The kingdom of God is as if someone would scatter seed on the ground, and would sleep and rise night and day, and the seed would sprout and grow, he does not know how.
>
> Mark 4:26–27

In both parables, growth is a divine mystery and a surprising reality. Seeds are scattered, and the fact that there is any growth at all is a bit remarkable. There is no mention of plowing or careful planting. The image is of a most careless gardener who tosses seeds here and there with many of the seeds falling onto ground that is unprepared to receive it. In these two parables, growth appears to be a complete mystery to the sower. It is as if growth occurs almost in spite of the sower's efforts. This seemed entirely consistent with what we were experiencing in Norwell. It was as if we were planting by day and somehow, almost as if it were happening while we were asleep, God was giving growth. If the lack of understanding in the text was disconcerting, what happened to the majority of the seeds sown was even more deeply troubling.

Lost Seeds

The parable of the sower speaks deeply of our experience of church growth and vitality in Norwell. In the parable, seeds were sown. Good seeds. It is not far-fetched to assume that somewhere there was likely many unnamed seeds planted in nice neat rows with plenty of room for plants to expand—that would only be expected. But in this parable, it was the seeds that fell to the ground by accident that seemed to make an impact. This is a very unsettling story in many respects, not least of which is that 75 percent of the seeds spoken of in the text is lost. Most of the seed were either eaten, scorched, or choked out. So we don't really know exactly how many seeds and effort were lost in this story. All we know is that most of the seeds sown or scattered or accidentally spilled produces nothing. And yet, as if by complete surprise or simple dumb luck, some seeds fall into receptive soil and the harvest turns out to be thirty, sixty, even one hundred times what was planted! Exponential growth comes where and when you least expected it. That was the parable, and it read like a page right out of our UCC Norwell story. It was as if the Holy Spirit refused to be controlled.

The message of the Spirit continued to encourage us, saying, "You just scatter the seeds, and leave the growth to me." This is not the most comforting message for people who like to be in charge, but it is the kind of miraculous response that has a way of inspiring faith.

As a pastor, even though it made me uncomfortable, this became my answer to church growth and vitality. Scatter seeds. Toss it everywhere. Cover the ground with the word of God. Don't leave a patch of earth unsown; then sit back and wait for the Holy Spirit to give growth. Marvel at the unexpected nature of where growth springs up. Learn to trust that even though much of our efforts will be lost, there will be an exponential increase somewhere that will be gloriously shocking in its impact on our community. That is exactly what is happening in our community, and to this day I go to bed not fully understanding it.

꼳 꼵

People, like seeds, can either remain unchanging in both mind and deed, or alternatively be open to the possibility of profound, transformational change. Churches with closed minds and hearts act safely within their comfort zones and tend to avoid challenges for fear of failing. Both individual and collective failure is experienced by the congregation as a reflection of inherent limitations that cannot be changed. People with closed minds and hearts behave like the seeds that fall on the path with no change, or on rocky places where the soil is shallow or among the thorns, and although growing quickly are unable to survive significant challenges. People with closed minds and hearts believe that their gifts and talents are basically unchangeable, give or take becoming a little bit better or a little bit worse over the course of a lifetime. Living with a closed mind and heart makes the journey through life a scary one. People feel threatened by negative feedback or criticism because the critics are assumed to be more knowledgeable and blessed with higher natural abilities.

People with open minds and hearts actively invite the Holy Spirit into their lives. Churches with open minds and hearts believe that their abilities can be improved by practice and therefore accept challenges as opportunities despite the risk of failure. People with open minds and hearts are not deterred by throwing their seeds on paths that are eaten by birds, or on rocky places, or even into thorns because they learn from each of these experiences. Both individual and collective failures are viewed as ways to stretch oneself and each other, to take more risks, to accept feedback, and ultimately to take the long-term view.

Many people live with fear that closes their minds and hearts. This fear leads people to quit after even one small failure because publicly revealing their failures to other people would be too painful and a manifestation of a lack of natural ability. As the body of Christ, we at UCC Norwell scatter many seeds on the ground. We scatter seeds in the work of preaching and teaching, at supporting each other, at serving others in need, and at creating more of God's kingdom here on earth. We have faith through an open mind and heart that God will eventually transform us, and like the seeds that falls on good soil, our blessings will multiply many times in the service of others.

Carl Isihara, Primary Care Internist and Former Moderator at UCC Norwell

꒫ ꒦

New Member Revelation

I see this kind of unexpected growth happening everywhere in our church. I see it when we take in new members. We average about thirty new members in a fall membership class, and when I sit down with them to assist them in their discernment about joining our community, I have come to know what to expect. I know that for one reason or another about ten of those new members will not remain in the community more than a year. I know that another third will think of themselves as truly committed church folks, but will only visit our congregation a couple of times a month—some no more than a couple of times a year. But then there will be another ten who will invest their lives in our community in ways that will be absolutely stunning and transform the life of our community by their presence in it.

What is most remarkable about this annual pattern of membership is that, even though I have watched as hundreds of new people have made their way into our church, while sitting with them in discernment, I still cannot tell who will fall into what category. There have been people who I was entirely convinced would make our church central to their lives who we rarely saw after that first year, while there are others I assumed were just passing through who have made an indelible imprint on our community by their personal and financial investment in it. There is always a thirty-, sixty-, one hundred-fold harvest from out of those membership classes; I just never know from which corner growth will spring up. Therefore, the only thing to do is to continue to scatter seeds everywhere we can.

Understanding the Soil

While I am one of those gardeners who can kill just about everything I plant, I do know that there are certain plant varieties that will not grow in the rocky New England soil in my backyard. A tomato plant will have a chance in my garden, whereas okra doesn't have a prayer. An apple tree might have a chance at surviving my care, while a banana tree will never be able to take root. I have a far better chance of harvesting cucumbers than I do kiwis.

Soil and climate are often dictating factors in what one can sow and what one can reap. Is it not possible that the same is true for the church? How a church can grow in Austin, Texas, is quite different from how a church can grow in Auburn, Maine. The primary reason is that the people in those locations are really different. A lifelong New Englander and a homegrown Texan may share the general human condition, but their life experiences and social histories can be worlds apart. There is truth to the motto that everything is big in Texas, while it is equally true that things can get a little chilly in New England. If the people are different, if the passions are different, if the politics are different, then it's a good bet that local churches will be different. The gospel may not change, but the prism through which the light of the gospel shines—the people—will reflect and refract in unique ways. As a result, there is no one-size-fits-all church. There is no patented formula for church growth. There is no standard model of ministry that will work well for every community.

The liberating truth of this reality is that pastors and the people they serve shouldn't worry about being like the huge church that is breaking new ground somewhere across the country. Nor do clergy and their churches need to feel as if they have to provide a spiritual buffet that meets everybody's needs all the time. Churches and their leaders should be free to be what Christ calls them uniquely to be, and leave the rest to the wisdom and movement of the Holy Spirit. When you know the particular gifts of the people, understand the unique character of the region, and trust that if you follow, Jesus will lead, church growth and vitality take root.

Great Expectations

Of course, what that growth and vitality look like is anyone's guess! When the Holy Spirit is in charge, anything can happen, for "the wind blows where it chooses, and you hear the sound of it, but you do not know where it comes from or where it goes" (John 3:8). For the pastor or the congregation that insists on being in control, surprising growth is anything but welcome. And yet, for those who are willing to embrace it, unpredictable growth that is prompted by the Spirit can be wildly exciting. I admit to initially being one of those pastors who liked knowing as much as possible about what was going on within my community. I liked having a plan, executing the plan, and reaping the harvest. However, the equation never quite worked out that way, so I wound up surrendering my need for a more predictable, gathered life, and now I find I revel in what the Holy Spirit might be up to next. This has not been an easy transition for me, but it has been an important one. As I tell pastors who ask me about engaging in ministry initiatives similar to the ones we employ in Norwell: You've got to be comfortable with a certain level of uncertainty that can seem at times to be bordering on chaos. Throwing seeds all over the place and praying for growth can seem like madness, particularly if you are the one doing the sowing. But, by the grace of God, it seems to work. We scatter seeds, and the Lord gives growth. That has become the new equation. It is an equation that simply doesn't add up. You lose 75 percent of the seeds you scatter, but the increase from the remaining 25 percent is thirty, sixty, one hundred times what you might expect.

꙳

Our answer to the perplexing questions of church vitality, particularly in regions where church growth is difficult business, is to keep throwing seeds on the ground trusting that the Holy Spirit will find a way to do something miraculous with it. Now I realize that some people may find this answer to be a cop-out, assuming that if we were better planners we would see even more impressive results. That may be true. Or perhaps our belief in scattering seeds and leaving the rest to God is a result of spiritual laziness. Some might accuse us of shirking our duty to nurture to maturity every single seedling that shows some progress and potential. I freely admit that, as a community, we probably fail in our calling as much as 75 percent of the time. But Scripture suggests we need things to work out right only one out of every four times for our efforts to be worthwhile. Whatever the case, whatever kind of ground the United Church of Christ in Norwell is, however modest our efforts to date, the Holy Spirit is doing something remarkable in our midst. In fact, the Holy Spirit has surprised us so many times in the past that I find I am always filled with great expectations about what will happen next. Scatter seeds and then wait to be surprised by the Spirit. That has turned out to be a very satisfying and faith-affirming way of cultivating church vitality.

Questions for Reflection

1. How would you describe your congregation's local character and flavor? What is the unique "soil and climate" of your community that influences the congregation's flavor?
2. What assumptions do you have, or have you had, about effective church growth and how it happens?
3. What is your congregation doing to reach new people? Have your efforts met with success? Why or why not?
4. On a scale of 1 to 10, what is your comfort level with uncertainty (1 being low need for control and certainty, 10 being high need for control and certainty)?
5. Think about your current congregational ministries and new efforts you are considering. How might you take a "tossing seeds everywhere" approach to these efforts?
6. Identify some ways in which tossing seeds everywhere and planning can work together.

CHAPTER 4

A Vital Theology

While it's true that UCC Norwell's basic approach is to cultivate congregational vitality and growth by tossing seeds *everywhere* and expect the Spirit's surprises, there is something more that accompanies that practice, something fundamental to the congregation's identity as seed sowers. Our life is centered on the person of Jesus Christ, and whoever you are, you are welcome to join us to explore that relationship. No one can enter our worship services without coming face to face with this core theological conviction.

DISCOVERING A NAME

I wasn't in seminary very long before I realized I was different, but I didn't have a name for what I was. I had grown up in two distinctly different religious worlds. My formal Christian education had taken place in the First Congregational Church in Fairport, New York, and was followed up by other traditional Presbyterian churches that we frequented when our family relocated. My more informal, and yet much more formational, Christian experience and education took place in small house-church gatherings that

my family and I participated in. At the big church in the center
of town, I learned the importance of corporate worship and community service. In the house-church gatherings, I learned about
personal faith and eternal salvation. The mainline churches of my
youth cultivated in me a desire for social justice and civic duty,
while in the house-church gatherings I learned to pray and to
study the Bible. Shuffling between these two different communities, I both fell in love with the church and believed passionately
in the Christian faith. One of the great joys of my childhood was
coming home from school and making my way up to my bedroom
to listen to the Bible story records my mother had given me. I had
learned the stories in church school and I had fallen in love with
the Bible in prayer circles.

As early I can remember, I possessed a faith that was distinc-
tively Christ-centered, while remaining open to the marvelous
complexity and creativity of God's creation. As I began to grapple
with my theological self-understanding in seminary, I found it
challenging to find a place where I fit in. The more liberal churches
that fed my social conscience seemed to exclude any reference to
Christ from their communal life, and the churches that strove to
be passionate followers of Jesus often seemed to exclude a whole
lot of people from their fellowship. I began to wonder if there was
a church for me, or if there was a new kind of church that I was
being called to help craft. In the midst of my confusion, a local pastor made a presentation to one of my seminary classes, and while I
have long forgotten the content of his lecture, I distinctly remember him referring to himself and to his church as both liberal and
evangelical. I had never heard those two words placed together as
if they belonged to one another, and yet from the moment they
were spoken in that class, I knew I had a term for who I was. I was
a *liberal* and *evangelical* Christian, and while much more to that
identity needed to be uncovered, I felt as if I had stumbled upon
language that began to express the faith that was burgeoning within me. The question that began to present itself in my mind was

whether or not there would be a congregation that would welcome a pastor whose beliefs and identity could seem so contradictory.

A LIBERAL AND EVANGELICAL CHURCH

I will never forget the moment as long as I live. I sat down with the Norwell search committee while I was looking for my next call. We had enjoyed engaging conversation, there was clearly some mutual interest in one another, and then one of the committee members uttered the phrase "UCC Norwell is a liberal and evangelical church." I was blown away. Tucked away in a little town I had never heard of before was a community of faith that was talking my language. While our conversation continued, in that moment I was sold. If a church could conceive of itself using terms similar to those I used to describe myself, then this had to be more than just a chance meeting. I began to suspect that we were meant for each other.

In the years that have followed, I am not sure the church was as liberal as it claimed to be, and I am fairly certain they didn't fully grasp how evangelical I was, but setting that aside, it has clearly been a good match. We have grown together, and we have grown in our understanding of our rather unique theological stance. Many people have asked what we mean when we term ourselves "liberal and evangelical." In truth, we probably don't fully understand our theological position. I have come to believe that liberal and evangelical theology and ethics is a bit of a moving target. However, by *evangelical* we tend to mean that we gather our community around the life, death, and resurrection of Jesus Christ, and we intend to share that story with anyone who will listen. By *liberal* we often mean that we believe that God's love is freely offered to everyone. We are a Christ-centered church and an Open and Affirming church. We invite Jesus into our community whenever two or three of us are gathered together, and we welcome gay, lesbian, bi-sexual, and transgendered people into our fellowship. We are a biblically based church that also strives to be socially progressive. We throw around multiple terms to explain who we are, or at least who we are striving to be, but in the end our attempt is to love Jesus and all his friends. This can prove to be a fairly precarious balancing act, but more often than not we pull it off with a fair degree of grace and generosity.

BUILDING ON THE CORNERSTONE

The New Testament attests that Jesus Christ is the cornerstone of Christian community. It is upon Jesus's life that our faith is built. Peter may be the rock of the church, but Jesus is the cornerstone. For years now, I have had a growing sense that a church community's health can directly relate to the presence of Jesus Christ in that community. I am certain there are plenty of exceptions, but when I have encountered struggling mainline churches, I have been struck by the lack of frequency with which Jesus is mentioned. Likewise, in communities where Jesus is central, there appears to be undeniable life and vitality. It cannot be a coincidence that mainline liberal Protestant denominations that tend to soft-pedal Jesus are in decline, while many Jesus-centered Christian churches and Christian faith movements that insist on a personal relationship with the Lord are thriving.

Among more liberal Christians, the aversion to Jesus Christ has little to do with Jesus himself and much more to do with the way more conservative or fundamental Christians tend to promote both Jesus and their faith. In these contexts, Jesus is seen as a symbol of exclusion at best, and an agent of bigotry at worst. Having spent years in more conservative Christian circles, I know firsthand that a focus on Christ can lead toward an exclusion and even contempt of others. I have heard more than my share of so-called Christ-centered sermons that have equated homosexuality, Islam, socialism, and a whole host of other issues and institutions as the work of the devil. That kind of narrow thinking repulses Christians who look at the story of the Last Supper—a central and sacramental Christian act—and recognize that Jesus invited to dinner the very people who would betray, deny, and desert him. How exclusive can Jesus be when that is the kind of company he was fond of keeping?

Instead of diving more deeply into the biblical text and challenging the assertions of the Christian right, the mainline liberal Protestant response has often been to untether itself from the Bible and to distance itself from Jesus. However, when you remove the cornerstone from the church, the institution itself can begin to crumble. Without the living Jesus at the heart of Christian community, the body begins to die. When we allow the Incarnate Word to become dusty or shelved entirely, biblical and relational illiteracy propels us again into an age when "the word of the LORD was rare in those days; visions were not widespread" (1 Sam. 3:1).

One of the initial attractions of UCC Norwell was that the fear of Jesus was not widespread. It would be inaccurate to assert that our church is a hotbed of evangelical fervor, but the community has demonstrated a steady willingness to keep the cornerstone of the church in place. When we assert that Jesus is not only the cornerstone of the community but also the head of the church, people don't get uncomfortable. I have come to believe that keeping Jesus central is at the heart of our church's vitality. The seeds we scatter are the gospel seeds that Jesus himself sowed from the Sea of Galilee to the city of Jerusalem. Jesus is the reason we plant in faith and reap in joy. New England may be a spiritually and culturally chilly place to try to cultivate Christian community, but the presence of Jesus has certainly warmed our fellowship.

INCLUDING ALL PEOPLE

UCC Norwell makes its home on the South Shore of Massachusetts in the heart of what Bostonians refer to as the Irish Riviera. As one might assume, this means that a significant percentage of our region's population have grown up Catholic. Roughly 60 percent of our church members have made the Catholic Church their spiritual home at one time or another. In short, the Catholic Church has been very good for the growth rate of our community. When I ask people why they left the Catholic Church to join our fellowship, their primary reasons are almost always the same—they felt excluded in their previous church. Communion was withheld, forgiveness was withheld, or affirmation was withheld. I still remember the first time my grandparents visited us for worship in Norwell. My grandparents were both Catholic, and because my grandmother had been divorced, her priest had prevented both of my grandparents from receiving communion. They hadn't been offered communion in more than thirty-five years. In advance of their visit, I told my deacons not to be concerned by the fact that my grandparents would remain seated while the rest of our congregation received the sacrament. However, the next week when my grandparents arrived for worship, after hearing our inclusive call to communion, my grandfather got out of his seat and began to walk forward. My grandmother quickly grabbed his arm and quietly requested to know what he was doing. In a voice loud enough for several congregation members to hear, my grandfather said, "There is no way I'm not accepting that invitation." After thirty-five years, both my grandparents received communion, and somehow the experience spoke to them about the all-embracing love of God that they had not felt for a very long time.

Issues of exclusion are hardly reserved for the Catholic Church. Conservative Christians set up as many barriers as anyone when it comes to welcoming people into Christ's church. I am not entirely sure why, but the more Jesus-focused a community of faith is, the more exclusive a community it tends to be. This leads many people who hunger deeply for faith to assume that all Christians are callous at best and downright bigoted at worst. There is a reason that white evangelical Christians and black evangelical Christians still have a fairly chilly relationship—it wasn't all that long ago that white evangelical Christians were citing passages of the Bible that they believed encouraged slavery and excluded civil rights.

Just as people can sense when the cornerstone of the church has been removed, folks can be downright alarmed when Jesus is presented as a divisive and exclusive figure. Too many people leave the church when they realize Christ is absent, and too many people are excluded from the church in the name of Jesus. I have always believed there must be a middle way that affirms the centrality of Christ while encouraging an extravagant love for all people. Liberals should be able to love Jesus, and evangelicals should be able to love Jesus's friends. At UCC Norwell, we aim to walk this middle way.

⚘ ⚘

"Liberal Evangelical . . . how can that be?" I've heard that said too many times.

I was raised in a very conservative, evangelical church. It was a loving congregation, but extremely "my way or the highway." Jews for Jesus were regular visitors. All outreach money was given to missionaries only. Love was abundant for everyone who agreed with the church's theology.

Then . . . I really rocked the boat—I married a Jew. My minister (a close family friend) refused to attend the ceremony.

With my conservative beliefs still in place despite my recent rocky journey, I stumbled upon a "Liberal Evangelical" church: UCC Norwell. Welcome homosexuals? That's not biblical. Support a non-denominational homeless shelter? Why not work to convert the homeless instead of supporting their lifestyle? The entire philosophy seemed an oxymoron to me: How can anyone be completely accepting of other's points of view and still believe in Jesus as your Lord and Savior?

It's been quite a journey. I've come to realize that the best example of a loving and accepting person is Jesus himself—and isn't he the "ultimate" Christian? It was explained to me that you can love Jesus AND his friends. I can accept others (faults, imperfections and all) and still profess Jesus as my Savior. I can love and welcome people who don't share my same beliefs, and if I truly listen to other's points of view, I can sometimes even change my mind! I can try to envision other's viewpoints and, whether or not I agree, welcome them into the church community. And welcome them completely—not as members that I hope to convert or change someday, but as Christians who believe in Jesus, who are imperfect like me, whose variety adds spice to our congregation.

Liberal Evangelical = Oxymoron? Maybe an oxymoron to those who believe that Jesus chose his friends carefully from the only best and most pious of His day.

Wendy Bawabe, graphic designer, mother, farmer, and
former clerk at UCC Norwell

❧ ❧

COMMUNION TABLE THEOLOGY

Easily the most important theological statement we make as a church is our call to the communion table. On the few instances when I have adjusted the words of invitation I speak, members of our community have approached me to tell me the effect of the missing words. They will often mention a visitor they noticed, or a member of the community they know who is in need of affirmation, or a family member who worships with them and longs to hear those words each week. As a result, the call to the communion table in our church rarely, if ever, changes. Looking out on the gathering of people, I speak these words: "This is the Lord's table, therefore the invitation to this table cannot come from a pastor, or a deacon, or any member of this community. The invitation comes from Jesus Christ, and it is always the same. 'Come as you are. It does not matter where you have been or where you are going, it doesn't matter what you have done or left undone, it doesn't matter whether you are feeling successful today, or whether you feel you have failed. There is always room at this table for you. The only thing you need to approach this table is a willingness to come forward. This is the Lord's table and you are invited to make it your table."

This serves as the heart and soul of our liberal and evangelical theology—Jesus is Lord, and you are welcome in his midst. Now we often have to remind people that a call to "come as you are" is not a mandate to "stay as you are." A relationship with Jesus should be a prelude to personal and social transformation. In fact, we often stress that you are invited to come as you are so that you can become the person God created you to be. Like all communities of faith, we fail in our mission on plenty of occasions, but the goal toward which we are aiming is undeniable. We follow Jesus Christ, and we welcome all people into that relationship with us.

ACCEPTING THE CONSEQUENCES

To be a liberal and evangelical church means to hold in tension theological perspectives that aren't easily yoked. It means having born-again Christians sitting in the same pew as gay and lesbian Christians. It means having Democrat and Republican church members sitting on boards and committees together. It means having active debates that can pit Christian education priorities against mission and justice priorities if budgets get tight. In a liberal and evangelical church, there are enough theological edges being pressed at one time that just about anyone can take offense at something. And yet, in the midst of that theological tension, we have found there is remarkable excitement. People can sense that our theology really matters and that we inhabit a unique and dynamic place in the American religious landscape. This does not mean that we don't chafe at the edges and that people don't become frustrated and leave. Due to the Christ-centered focus of our congregastion, we have lost most of our Unitarian members over the past decade. I still remember a conversation with a couple who angrily made a beeline to my office after a Sunday morning service. They were viscerally upset by an anthem our cherub choir had sung that morning. Our children had given voice to lyrics that stated that through the blood of Jesus Christ our sins are washed clean. I still remember the husband, red in the face, with veins bulging in his neck, demanding to know why children had to sing about such violent images and beliefs. They both wondered why the church couldn't get past Jesus Christ and the theology of the cross. I have long since forgotten the answer I gave them, but it did not prevent them from leaving our community shortly thereafter.

However, as a fairly orthodox Christian church, there are theological lines we refuse to cross. Excluding Jesus and the memory of his suffering from our community are a couple of them. Since we live in Massachusetts, our congregation leans to the left politically, and therefore our church has a decidedly liberal slant on most issues that afflict our world. We unabashedly believe that God's love is intended to be spread liberally throughout the world. While I can't remember the specific sermon, one Sunday evening one of our Republican church members informed me that he, and other politically conservative members of our church, might choose to be absent for a few Sundays as a silent protest to a comment I had made while preaching. I had referenced some theological concerns about the social stances of "conservative Christians" and a number of my church members had taken offense. It turned out to be an issue of poor communication, because most of the conservative Christians at UCC Norwell are conservative politically but fairly liberal when it comes to matters of theology. We have Christians who happen to be socially or politically conservative, but very few who would be traditionally defined as Conservative Christians. As one might imagine, language has been a challenge for us. We don't always know how to speak about who we are and what we believe; therefore, there are moments when offense is taken. The only way through a theological briar patch like this is for the pastor and people to trust that the love and care between them is real and ultimately sustaining.

A FORCE FOR GROWTH AND VITALITY

Early on in my ministry in Norwell, I was describing all the different organizational and program changes we were making to a former professor of mine from Boston University. With great enthusiasm I described our new ministry team model, our streamlined governance structure, and our focus on people feeling called to ministry instead of being guilted into the work of the church. I raved about our commitment to service, our commitment to youth ministry, and our passion for people to understand their lives for ministry. My professor friend looked bemused as I bubbled over with hope and optimism for my new church. After I concluded my report, he waved his hand dismissively and said, "You'll come up with a new structure and model for ministry in five years when your current model breaks down . . . It is your theology that makes your church unique and exciting. Theology will fuel your church's growth." I remember feeling a bit deflated at this comment because of my awareness of the many hours of prayer, discernment, discussion, and visioning that had gone into the process of restructuring the organizational life of our church. And yet, the truth of this statement has been borne out in the years that have followed.

No one who enters our community for the first time—or even for the first year for that matter—cares about our Ministry Team structure, or our commitment to personal sharing before getting down to the business of a particular team, or our creative style of governance that frees people up to follow their call to ministry. It is our theology that people first encounter as they walk through our doors. What a stunning revelation—theology really matters! When people enter a community of faith, they want to know what that community believes. An individual cannot enter our services of worship without coming face-to-face with our core theological convictions: Our life is centered on the person of Jesus Christ, and whoever you are you are welcome to join us to explore that relationship. Name tags, a warm greeting at the door, and pastoral visits to newcomers are helpful elements in a church's desire to be invitational in nature, but for people to enter a community, stay in that community, and grow as a part of that community, theology really counts. Living in this somewhat unusual intersection between liberal social concerns and a more orthodox Christology has turned out to be a very exciting theological location to inhabit.

We at UCC Norwell have recognized the uniquely important opportunity we have—an opportunity for radical discipleship that witnesses to the power of love to unite people across ideological and theological lines. This book only begins to scratch the surface of the theological stance that has propelled much of our growth as a community of faith. Dr. Wesley Wildman and I have written two volumes dedicated to a much more in-depth study of the theology and ethics of liberal and evangelical Christianity. Our first book, *Lost in the Middle? Claiming an Inclusive Faith for Christians Who Are Both Liberal and Evangelical,* directly addresses a very large group of moderate Christians, especially in the United States. Our second volume, *Found in the Middle! Theology and Ethics for Christians Who Are Both Liberal and Evangelical,* focuses on the challenges that arise when Christians of this passionately moderate sort find each other and gather together in congregations.[1]

For the seeds of church vitality to take root and grow, a vital theology is essential: It not only defines the identity of the sowers, but also guides us as we tend the growth.

Questions for Reflection

1. What theology defines your congregation? Can you state it in one or two sentences?

2. In what ways does your congregation's central theology come through your worship? your newsletter, website, and other internal and external communication? other congregational activities? Where are the gaps? What communication methods need to be strengthened?

3. Invite several people from other congregations to identify the theological messages they hear in your worship, read in your congregational communications, or perceive when they participate in your congregation's activities. (You might offer to do the same thing for their congregation.)

PART 3

Tending Growth

CHAPTER 5

Ministry Teams

In addition to scattering seeds in all kinds of soil, we also recognize and claim our role of tending the growth that God gives. In this nurturing role, it is the people of the congregation who are the ministers, and the pastor's role is to tend to the people. From its earliest days up to the present, the people of UCC Norwell have claimed this central responsibility.

THE DILEMMA

Before my arrival at UCC Norwell, the congregation had plans underway to revamp its organizational structure. Their experience was one that is true for so many Christian communities today: Too few people are doing too much work in the church. Church leaders, both lay and ordained, grow older and grayer and they eventually burn out. That had become the situation at the United Church of Christ in Norwell toward the end of the twentieth century. The church was only a few decades old, but the organizational structure had become a burden that fewer and fewer people were willing to bear. The church had significant lay participation in worship, in youth ministry, and in mission work, but the boards and committees that oversaw the day-to-day operations of the church were slowly breaking down. The nominating committee had to call people up and beg them to join church boards. The sales pitch was nearly desperate: "Will you please, please, please join the trustee board? No one else wants to do it." Needless to say, that is not an effective means of drawing in new members.

The truth was that the different boards and committees were so overburdened with tasks that any sense of fellowship and passionate mission was drained out of them. The deacons, for example, were responsible for worship, which included setting up for services, serving communion, leading worship, designing special services, finding and training ushers and greeters, decorating the sanctuary for the different liturgical seasons, and making sure that the church had enough palms on Palm Sunday and enough candles on Christmas Eve—just to list a few of their liturgical responsibilities. The deacons were also responsible for following up on church members who were absent from church, collecting the names and addresses of people who visited the church on a weekly basis, running new member classes, and making sure that coffee was available for fellowship hour each Sunday after worship. The tasks lacked a central focus, and the board members lacked passion for their work. In fact, it felt as if any miscellaneous task the church needed done but didn't have a proper home for fell to the deacons. This was true for many of our boards and committees.

Additionally, because the different task groups were already maxed out with their load of commitments, this meant that starting new ministries was not something that could be freely considered or encouraged. Even if the church could find enough leaders for its board and committee structure, the structure itself was preventing ministerial innovation and growth. If that was not bad enough, because all board and committee chairs had a seat on the church council, few people wanted the position because of that additional commitment. When it was time to identify a new chair for a board, the person selected was typically the person who forgot to step backward when volunteers were asked to step forward. As one might imagine, not only did this weaken individual boards and committees, but it weakened the church council—the primary governing body in the church—because many of the folks who made up that central leadership team didn't really want to be there.

Thankfully, a couple of years before I began my ministry in Norwell, the church began a process of reenvisioning it's structural and institutional life. A task force was formed with the explicit instruction to develop a new way of gathering around the varied tasks of the community. A church consultant was brought in to help energize the imaginations of the congregation. Project 2000, as it was called, was launched . . . and shortly thereafter a new pastor was called.

RELATIONSHIPS AND DISCERNING CALL

Project 2000 was a multiphased structural visioning process that took several years and numerous task forces to complete. As different iterations of purpose and vision statements were drafted and adopted, as core values were identified and tested, and as structural adjustments were proposed, important themes began to emerge. Early on, these different task forces began to sense that the purpose of gathering people together in the structural life of the community needed to be more than just about completing a task. People rarely felt called to tasks, but almost always made room for relationships. Biblical reflection seemed to bear out that God's desire to work with people to accomplish divine purposes was evidence that tasks were merely a means of entering into important relationships. If the work of the church was going to have any connection to the work of God, then the tasks in which the church engaged had to be primarily about relationships—relationships with God and relationships with one another. You can pick up faint traces of this theme in both of the statements that different task forces framed for the church:

> *We are an inclusive community seeking to connect the gospel message to our everyday lives. We seek a church that is more than a geographical place, more than a gathering of people, more than a program and organization. We seek a sacred center, a sense of Sabbath, a community that empowers us for our daily ministries.*
>
> Project 2000 Phase Two Task Force.

> *We are a Christ-Centered, inclusive community, called to ministry.*
>
> 2003 Visioning Task Force

The need to cultivate the life of the community and deepen our relationship with Jesus Christ were clear themes in the visioning work of all phases of Project 2000. Building Christian community was the first priority of the church; task accomplishment would be a somewhat distant second. This came to mean that the *how* of our gatherings was more important that the *what* of our time together. The *way* we gathered was of greater importance than *what we did* when we gathered. If teams were going to gather around particular tasks, then we had to set some expectations for how community could be more deeply cultivated while engaging in the work of the church.

The various Project 2000 task forces also began to sense that people should be prompted to ministry inside and outside the church, not by a sense of guilt but by careful discernment of call. In short order, the work of Project 2000 demonstrated the need to have a call-based organizational structure. If we were going to engage in a particular ministry, we would do so because a group of people felt truly called by God to engage in that work. We would no longer engage in ministries simply because we had always done so. If we were going to be a call-based church, we had to honor the fact that we might be called *away* from long-standing ministries that we had always deemed essential. This was one of the most significant leaps of faith our community took in the whole restructuring process.

As is the case with most churches, our community is quite reluctant to give up long-standing ministries, even if there aren't enough people to support them. Moving to a call-based structure would potentially require some letting go. Following this line of thinking, we had to grapple with the possibility that if we did not have anyone stepping forward to teach fourth-grade church school, perhaps, as a community we were not called to offer fourth-grade church school. If no one felt called to make and serve coffee after worship, perhaps we were not called to have coffee at Fellowship Hour. If no one felt called to join Women's Fellowship, perhaps we were no longer called to that particular ministry. This was a challenging ethic to consider implementing. How could a church not have fourth-grade church school, or coffee, or Women's Fellowship? What would it mean if no one felt called to be a deacon, or a trustee, or a member of the finance board? The church could literally fall apart!

These very real fears began to point to our need to trust in the Holy Spirit's ability to form community, more than in our need to fill boards and committees. We began to suspect that the crisis we were facing was not a crisis of structure, but a crisis of faith. Whose work were we really trying to do? Did we really believe that the fortunes of the church rose and fell primarily by our own efforts? Did we assume our nominating committee was the only force for recruitment within the church? During this time I began to feel fairly passionate about letting the Holy Spirit take a greater hand in the running of UCC Norwell. If Jesus Christ was truly alive and active in the world, perhaps he could lead his church better than we could. If the church was only focused on doing what we wanted to do, instead of trying to discern what God wanted us to do, perhaps our most faithful action would be to shutter the church and join a secular civic organization instead. Of all the many blessings of

Project 2000, one of the most pronounced gifts was the realization that the church was entrusted to our stewardship, but it belonged to Jesus Christ. If we were going to be faithful to Christ's call on our community, then we needed to trust in the Holy Spirit's ability to call individual members of our church into service.

Rules for Teams

Through our own research into new and emerging models of ministry, we began to explore the possibility of transitioning the boards and committees within our church into ministry teams. We would gather into intentional teams that would make an ongoing commitment to come together not only to engage in the work of the church but also to serve as smaller communities of support and care within our church. We went about setting some guidelines for how our teams might be established and run.

First, noting that Jesus and the early church always sent disciples out two by two, we decided that if our ministry was to be truly team-based, then people couldn't be in ministry alone. To engage in a ministry within our church, there had to be at least two people feeling called to a particular effort. There would no longer be any Lone Rangers within our church. In an attempt to encourage the invitational nature of ministry teams, we agreed that all team gatherings would always have an empty chair as a part of any gathered circle of members. The empty chair was meant both to symbolize the presence of Jesus Christ in our midst and to remind ministry teams to always be thinking about who they might invite into their ministry. To engage in a ministry, an individual had to be part of a team. If a team could not be gathered around a particular ministry, then that would be an indication that our church was not called to engage in that particular work. This meant that for a ministry team to take shape, it needed to be examined and approved by the governing council of the church. Receiving council approval is not arduous, but it is an important regulatory process. The council's responsibility is to make sure that teams function within the framework of our mission while conforming to the expectations we have for our ministry teams. While it was clear from the beginning that ministry teams were going to be afforded great freedom in their ability to pursue the call God placed upon people's hearts, the council would still have oversight to ensure that teams were functioning in line with the core mission and values of our community.

Next, we realized that for a team to be formed with people who felt called to a particular ministry meant that the laundry list of tasks that our current boards and committees had taken on over the years needed to be set aside, and perhaps even entirely discarded in some cases. Ministry teams were going to be much more narrowly focused. If you felt called to support the worship life of the church as a deacon, you were not going to be asked to call on church members that hadn't been to church recently. If you felt called to serve as an usher, you were not going to have to worry about making coffee. If you felt called to work with youth, you were not going to have to spend every waking hour coming up with curriculum for children's church school. *Focus* was going to be a key feature of these new teams. In fact, as we contemplated this transition, we realized that a single board or committee might have to break into several ministry teams in order to fit into our new model of ministry.

Most important, when teams gathered, they needed to take an extended time to share their lives with one another. No longer would church meetings begin with the sharing of a perfunctory prayer or poem, only to dive right into the evening's business agenda. Rather, teams were asked to take unhurried time to check in with one another about what was going on in their respective lives. The rule for this time of sharing was that there was to be no cross talk, people were encouraged to speak about their lives without comment or critique from others. We hoped this would free people to speak honestly and openly without being concerned about the opinions or biases of others. Relationships would come first; business would come afterward. We kept asking ourselves, "How can we truly be in ministry with one another if we don't really know each other?" The answer, of course, was that we couldn't. We quickly developed an expectation that teams would focus on sharing and a time of prayer at the beginning of the meeting as if it was the most pressing agenda item. Some other item might fall off the agenda before any sharing time was sacrificed.

For teams that maintain this commitment, we find that once the time of sharing and praying is over, the team tends to fly right through the task list to be discussed. I suspect this is because some of the baggage that we bring into our meetings—the challenges we have faced during the day—can often sidetrack conversation as we begin to address issues that can be potentially contentious. If team members have felt listened to and cared for in the time of sharing, then it becomes less likely they will argue over where to place the Christmas concert sign on the front lawn.

We also decided that if we were going to allow the Holy Spirit to call people forward into ministry, then we shouldn't have a nominating committee trying to harangue people into service. We decided that ministry teams would be self-nominating, and anyone who wanted to join a team simply needed to show up and commit to staying with the team for at least a year. In fact, in a desire to be open to the call of the Spirit, we decided to allow non-members of our community to join in our teams, whereas boards and committees had formerly been comprised of official church members. No term limitations were placed on members of teams, so individuals who wanted to join a particular ministry could do so freely and stay on board as long as that calling captured their spirit and filled them with passion.

This new way of doing ministry seemed daring, and it was so different from the previous four decades of ministry that we had many concerns. We needed a way to begin, a way to test our ideas before deciding to implement them churchwide. We knew we would make plenty of mistakes and missteps, so we decided to start slowly before accelerating the process. We began by piloting our new model for ministry with one of our most overburdened boards. After several months of rigorous discernment, our deacon board became our first official ministry team—or more accurately, the deacons transitioned into six different ministry teams. Thus, our structural transition was launched.

DEACON PILOT TEST

While our deacon board was tired and longed to be unburdened of many of its responsibilities, the work of letting go of previous commitments proved challenging. As is often the case in any church, people are reluctant to stop working on a particular ministry if they worry that there won't be anyone to take it up again. So it was with much hand and heart wringing that the deacons began to set aside tasks to which they no longer felt called. This process actually began with the deacons trying to claim tasks to which they *did* feel called. It took quite some time, but the deacons came to the conclusion that ensuring the care and integrity of the church's worship experience was their primary, and perhaps, only role. They would be responsible for all the nuts and bolts of the worship service: preparing the sanctuary, preparing and serving communion, making sure that candles were lit, and that the gathered people had the worship resources they needed. Not surprisingly, the very first ministry they let go of was one they had never had much time to tend to: worship planning.

With the church council helping to call forward church members to the tasks the deacons were letting go of, a worship planning ministry team was launched. This was a team that would focus primarily on planning the flow and liturgy of our worship service, while the deacons would focus on actually making it happen. If there was an adjustment to be made to the format of worship, if an additional worship service needed to be crafted, and if themes were desired for the different liturgical seasons of the year, the worship planning ministry team was going to be in charge of it. This was work that the deacons would have enjoyed attending to and may have felt called to, but they never had time for.

As it turned out, there were more than enough church members who wanted to have a hand in crafting worship, so the new ministry team formed quickly and with great enthusiasm. With that success behind them, the deacons began to spin off other ministries. They created a membership development ministry team to tend to the new members and the absent members of the community. They created a sound room ministry team that took care of the audiovisual aspects of worship. They created an ushers ministry team. And, finally, they prepared to launch the coffee and greeters ministry team. This turned out to be the most difficult team to form. Up until that point, every time the deacons spun off a ministry into another team, some members of the deacon team felt called to join the new team and help in the early stages of transition. No such interest was found when it came to making the coffee on Sunday mornings. Except for the worship planning ministry team, which came together rather effortlessly, each of the other ministry teams took shape somewhat tenuously, with the deacons worrying that no one would step forward to take on the ministry. The deacons feared transitioning out of particular responsibilities and then watching them go untended. The anxious mantra of the deacons was "What if no one feels called to lead the ushers?" "What if no one feels called to work in the sound room?" "What if no one feels called to run our Inquirers classes for new members?" It seemed as if each time the deacons let go of a ministry, they thought that ministry might die of neglect. However, seemingly just in the nick of time, as the deacons finally let go of a particular ministry, a group of people gathered around the task and a new team was formed.

But no one came forward to make the coffee. The deacons hated making the coffee for Sunday morning, but they couldn't imagine fellowship hour without it. With wavering resolve and an even shakier faith, the deacons finally decided to stop making coffee. Bracing themselves for the fallout, the Sunday came when the deacons didn't set out our coffee service, and that Sunday we had fellowship hour after worship without a single cup of coffee being poured. The deacons felt terrible, they felt as though they had let the congregation down. They disliked making the coffee, it didn't feel like a responsibility the deacons should have, but they didn't like disappointing the congregation either. What was to be done?

The following Monday morning, a longtime church member came to the church office and announced that coffee was an essential part of church fellowship and that she and a friend wanted to form a ministry team to meet that need. Thus, the coffee and greeters ministry team was born, and we have been called as a community to make coffee ever since.

With the successful transition of the deacon board to ministry teams, the church voted in January of 2002 to adopt the ministry team organizational model as the new structural norm for the church. If we were called to a particular ministry, we would engage in that ministry as part of a team, and we would spend as much time nurturing the life of the team and the individuals on it as we did the tasks we were gathered to perform. Since that vote, our church has birthed numerous ministry teams and our community has experienced a renewed enthusiasm for the work of the church. Perhaps this was in part because our new model implicitly affirmed that the primary work of the church was to build community. People aren't drawn to tasks as passionately as they are drawn to relationships, and the ministry team model is inherently relational. Our model was not perfect, and it has plenty of flaws to this day, but the call to team-based ministry is a call we are committed to. It is biblically grounded, it further deepens relational connections, and tasks are accomplished without a sense of guilt or burden. Ministry teams have not been our salvation, but they

have turned out to be a very effective means of tending to the work
of our church.

⚘ ⚘

Coffee, coffee , coffee. Regular or decaf ? Styrofoam, plastic, or pa-
per cups? Who would order it? Who would make it? Who would
serve it? How many cups should we make? What pots should we
use? Should we purchase carafes? Who would clean up?

It doesn't seem to be a controversial topic that would generate lengthy hours of discussion at a monthly deacons' meeting,
but added to the laundry list of tasks assigned or taken on by default, there was rarely time for consideration of the core mission
of the deacons, which was the worship life of the congregation.

In addition to coffee, deacons manned the sound room, re-
cruited greeters each Sunday, arranged for ushers, and oversaw
the flower, music , and New Beginnings sub committees (with a
deacon liaison attending each of their meetings and reporting
back at our meeting). Deacons decorated for Christmas, replaced
candles, attended council, prepared and served communion.
They met with prospective new members and officiated with
pastors on membership Sundays and baptisms. Deacons end-
lessly discussed membership issues, including how to promote
the church in the community, encourage visitors to become
weekly participants, and revitalize attendance among the current members. Churchwide small groups were organized, work-
shops with guest speakers offered, retreats planned, etc. These
all needed . . . guess what? Coffee.

When the idea of ministry teams evolved from Project 2000,
the board of deacons enthusiastically volunteered to pilot the
concept. Something had to be done to share the overwhelming
tasks and allow deacons to identify and keep what they most
valued. Ministry teams would emerge because of a special interest in keeping or developing an area of need. The idea of being "called" to a ministry helped congregants think about their
strengths and interests and about where God was calling them

to serve without concern of a set term of office. More people then would serve on the various teams and some might choose to serve on more than one team.

Serving as a deacon became about serving communion rather than coffee.

Barbara Engstrom, Consulting teacher of reading and former deacon chair at UCC Norwell

꒦ ꒦

MODERATOR TEAM AND COUNCIL

As we began our transition to a new team-based model for ministry, one of the most helpful changes was in our church's governing council. In previous years, the church council had been led by a moderator, a vice moderator, a few other officers, some at-large members, and then the board and committee chairs of the church's various ministries. While this model of governance had worked for decades, we could see stress and fraying around the edges. The presiding moderator always had an enormous amount of work to do; in fact, in times of crisis certain moderators found themselves so overwhelmed by the work of the church that their vocational lives outside the church suffered or, in one case, had to be put on hold. The demands on the moderator were so evident and daunting that oftentimes the vice moderator would have no interest in filling the role once the presiding moderator's term was up. Given the weight of the role, it was always a daunting task to try to identify new moderators and to get them to commit to a three-year term. However, the greatest challenge to the efficacy of the church council was the board and committee chairs who made up most of the gathered body. Board and committee chairs were often chosen by default. No one else wanted the job, so that board or committee member who objected least strenuously was often given the role. After being appointed to the chair of a particular board or committee, the new chairperson would learn, to their dismay, that they were also required to go to church council meetings. This often led to a less than enthusiastic or downright absent church council membership. Being on the church council was viewed as another burden and not as an opportunity to engage in thoughtful discernment that could offer the congregation important direction.

Our Project 2000 transition into a team-based model of ministry was every bit as radical for the church council as it was for our boards and committees. We made the decision to have a team of three moderators who would work together in successive terms. We would have an incoming moderator, who, in their first year with the council would be responsible for keeping track of our ministry teams through the council's coordinating committee (see "Untethered Balloons and Commication Issues"). The convening moderator, who was in their second year with the council, would be responsible for running the church council and all congregational meetings throughout the year. The outgoing moderator, who was in their final year with the council, would be responsible for all active task forces that the church council had established. Distinct from ministry teams, task forces would organize around short-term goals, and when those were accomplished, the task force would disband. The three moderators would meet with pastoral staff on a regular basis to deal with any pressing issues facing the congregation and to prepare for the monthly council meeting.

Of all the transitions we have made over the past ten years, expanding from one moderator into a moderator ream has been one of the most helpful developments in our life together. No longer do moderators feel as if they are carrying the burden of church leadership on their own. No longer do pastoral staff members feel as though they are working with an overburdened layperson. And no longer are unrealistic burdens placed on any one person. Again, our ministry needed to be team-based on every level because ministry shouldn't be done alone.

The other advance we made in our governing structure was to eliminate the need to have board and committee chairs on the council. At-large members of the council would now be selected solely for their ability and desire to help discern direction for the community. Sitting on the church council would be its own task; it would not be an added commitment for a less than enthusiastic board or committee chair. People who felt truly called to church governance would be able to focus specifically on that task.

We also committed to treating our moderator team and the church council as a ministry teams themselves. That meant sharing and community building within those teams was paramount. Since this transition, the improvement of the spirit and efficacy of the church council has been remarkable. The council is focused, people feel honored to be invited into leadership roles, and we are much more productive as a team. The church council is also a much stronger body, with much more authority in the life of the church.

Untethered Balloons and Communication Issues

There was one nagging problem in our leadership transition that took us several attempts to effectively address. When our new ministry model was diagrammed on newsprint for our church leaders to see, there was a central bubble that said "Church Council," and then there were twenty to thirty smaller surrounding bubbles with the names of all our new ministry teams in them. Jerry Thornell, a longtime member and church leader, looked at the diagram and said, "This looks like a bunch of balloons with no strings attaching them to anything. What are they going to attach to? Or will this model simply allow these teams to float away on their own?"

Whatever our response was on that particular night, we went ahead with our untethered ministry model, and ever since, our greatest challenge has been to keep track of teams that are prone to floating off into the wild blue yonder.

By eliminating the responsibility of board and committee chairs to sit on the church council, we severed the traditional line of communication between church leadership and the many other ministries the church engages in. Anticipating that loss, we came up with the idea of having a coordinating committee made up of all the at-large members of the council who would serve as liaisons to the different ministry teams and attend team meetings when it was feasible. The coordinating committee would then report to the church council if there were any pressing issues that the ministry teams needed the church council to address. This sounded good in concept, but it was an absolute failure in practice. There were too many ministry teams for the coordinating committee to effectively manage, and the at-large council members quickly became frustrated with their inability to keep in contact with the different teams. Part of the challenge was that ministry teams were allowed to meet whenever they could find a time that worked for them, so a council member could have been out every night of the week attending ministry team meetings. Before long, it was evident that council members were not connecting with their teams, and the teams began to feel as if they were losing touch with the church council.

Our immediate response was to invite two of our most vital and active ministry teams to have a seat on the church council if they so chose. To this day, a member of our mission and outreach ministry team, and a member of our trustee's ministry team will show up at our monthly council meetings.

The second attempt to find ways for the coordinating committee to effectively serve as liaisons to all the ministry teams was through an evening gathering when leaders of a couple of ministry teams, and sometimes entire teams themselves, would meet with the coordinating committee. Instead of having at-large members of the council go to ministry team meetings, the ministry teams would be expected to go to the coordinating committee meetings. In theory, over a sixth-month period, all of the ministry teams would be able to be seen and heard by the coordinating committee. This assumed, of course, that ministry teams needed only two meetings a year to feel connected to the church council and the wider mission of the church. Again, we met with failure. Between our two attempts at coordinating our untethered teams, enough time had elapsed that communication within the church as a whole began to break down. The church council and the ministry teams had virtually no idea what the other was doing. While the ministry teams were functioning well and maintaining their enthusiasm, the balloons were drifting all over the place, and the church structure was beginning to feel a bit more chaotic than anyone was comfortable with.

Then, to our surprise, we were confronted by a pastoral transition that wound up providing us an opportunity to address the disconnection between council leadership and our ministry teams. We temporarily found ourselves in a situation where we only had one pastor, and there was no way that one pastor could provide the pastoral support ministry teams needed. We knew that some new and decisive measures were needed. We decided to make a request that all ministry teams that felt they needed more pastoral and council support start attending an "All Church Meeting Night" on the second Tuesday of the month. Pastoral staff, the incoming moderator, and all the at-large members of the church council would be present for "All Church Meeting Night." We would gather church leadership and ministry teams together for a brief time of worship, we would give a focused sharing question for all the teams to use, and at-large council members would sit with the different teams and then report back to the council at the end of the month if there were particular issues that needed to be addressed. If a certain ministry team didn't feel the need to meet regularly on

All Church Meeting Night, that was acceptable; however, all teams would be required to attend All Church Meeting Night at least a couple of times a year to ensure that the church council understood the ministries the teams were engaging in.

It took three attempts, but we finally struck upon a way of tethering the balloons together so that none of them accidentally floated away only to be forgotten. I wish I could say that communication between our ministry teams and our church council is now perfect, but that would not be true. There are teams that still slip through the cracks. There are teams that rarely if ever meet with council members, and there are still too many teams for any one person—or any one pastor—to keep track of. However, communication is vastly improved, the church council feels fairly well informed, and ministry teams generally feel supported by leadership. While communication issues continue to be the greatest challenge to our model of ministry, the struggle for teams to be well connected is mitigated by the unqualified success of the teams themselves. This is not to say that the ministry teams themselves haven't encountered issues that we did not anticipate when our model of ministry was initially approved by our congregation. As is always the case in Christ's church, as our ministry continues, new issues always arise. Thankfully we have learned to embrace these issues as opportunities for further growth as a community.

CONTINUING CRACKS IN THE SYSTEM

In a spirit of full disclosure, and in the hope that other faith communities will be able to avoid some of the pitfalls we have experienced, it is important to share a few of the other challenges that team-based ministry continually presents us with. These issues are not overwhelming and they do not make us question the viability of our model, but they are issues that appear to be with us indefinitely.

One of the most significant challenges had to do with the process of nominating people to the different ministry teams. Our ministry model was designed for all of our teams to be self-nominating. The idea was that enthusiastic ministry teams and team members would be their own best advocates, and their desire to invite people to join them in ministry would be infectious. This has not been the case. Our ministry teams rarely, if ever, think to add new members, and when they do think about inviting other people in, they rarely follow through. Part of the issue is that busy people have a difficult time asking other busy people to join them in doing more work. Even if the time will be spent in a form of community building, team members are reluctant to ask for people to volunteer. Therefore, teams slowly but surely lose members as people transition off the teams, and within a relatively short period of time, teams find themselves saddled with more work than the team can handle. Our rejuvenated church structure allowed ministry teams to enthusiastically engage in their ministries, but those teams never fully embraced their nominating and recruiting role. Thus, team strength eventually dwindles to a critical level. No matter the amount of encouragement, our teams do not self-nominate effectively. Therefore, the task of recruiting new members falls to pastoral and program staff. While the ministry model has many benefits, it has forced our pastoral and program staff to spend a significant amount of time on team building. For our model of ministry to work, pastoral and program staff always need to be engaged in the process of helping church members discern their call to ministry within the church. I had no idea how much of my job would be focused on recruitment and team building. There is no question that team building is the most significant area of growth for pastoral and program staff since adopting our new organizational model. It would appear essential for a pastor to have significant recruitment gifts for this model of ministry to be successful.

Another issue that we have had to deal with is the thorny issue of problematic team members. As is the case in so many churches, if a difficult church member was nominated to a particular board or committee, the board or committee members simply suffer through their term and, at the end of three years, the difficult team member would transition off the team and would never be asked back. This meant that challenging personality conflicts could be swept under the carpet, and in the desire to be polite, inappropriate behavior was never addressed. Now that ministry team members can stay on their teams as long as they feel called to be there, there is no way to procedurally graduate problematic members from the team. This leaves teams with two options. First, and least painful, is for team members to simply become frustrated with difficult personalities and leave the teams themselves. Rather than dealing directly with difficult situations, individuals can respond to the challenge by surrendering their call to a particular ministry. In truth, this option is utilized more frequently than any of us in local churches might like to admit.

The second option is to directly address behavior that hampers the team. Even though it is clearly the uncomfortable route to take, I am glad that with greater regularity, teams are choosing to work through difficult relational issues directly rather than fleeing from them. This presents us with an opportunity, as daunting as it might be, to more fully live out our Christian calling to be in full communion with one another and with our God. When we are forced to be truthful with one another, while striving to be generous and caring with one another, relationships are deepened. It is often the case that when uncomfortable subjects are broached in a spirit of love, people find they are drawn more closely together rather than torn apart. In unexpected ways, our ministry teams force us to be more faithful in our relationships with one another than we are generally accustomed to being.

The other significant ministerial issue we have had to deal with is the assumption that God's call on our lives is synonymous with following our bliss. This belief suggests that if I like doing something, or if I derive pleasure from a particular task, then I must be called to it. Conversely, if there is a task I find difficult or unpleasant, I must not be called to it. In our attempt to free people from the guilt of serving the church, the pendulum swung with great force in the other direction. While offering people the freedom to say no to particular tasks in the church was liberating in many important ways, the consequences of that freedom quickly turned out to be a rather one-dimensional sense of call. We needed to really stress that "call" is not just about "doing things you like to do." We took the cross as our focal point and began to talk about call requiring sacrifice. In fact, we went so far as to say that if there is no sacrifice present in a particular endeavor in an individual's life, then that may be an indication that it is not God's call for that person. God's call on our lives is certainly joyous, but God's call is also costly, and almost always requires significant sacrifice. It was true for Jesus; therefore, it should be true for us.

While these challenges to our new model for ministry were unanticipated by our church and difficult to work through, they have offered us important opportunities to reflect upon and refine our structural life. I have found that each and every new work in our church has required a time of adjustment. We never make a plan that works out just the way we had envisioned it. Perhaps it is a great blessing that we have as many failures as we have successes; therefore, we are continually reminded that we must rely of Christ's guidance for our life together. As a church we cannot do this ministry on our own . . . we need Jesus.

COMMUNITY BUILDING

Having experienced both the blessings and the challenges of ministry teams, I remain not only a fan but an advocate for this organizational model. I have come to believe that everything that is done in the life of the church is about building community. The music ministry team's focus should not be about producing a flawless

Christmas concert, but it should find ways to build community through rehearsal and performance. The trustee ministry team's primary interest should not be about ensuring the most cost-effective approach to facility maintenance, but rather should be about how our building promotes fellowship. A prayer shawl ministry team gathering should be as intent on caring for one another as they are about stitching baby blankets and comfy throws. The reason for having any church structure at all is to help enhance and secure the welfare of the community. Staff, the church council, ministry team members, and other lay leaders should understand that their work is foundationally about relationship. The sharing and caring that we have witnessed through our ministry team model is evidence that our organizational structure is helping us to pursue our most sacred task—cultivating Christ's community in the world.

While our team-based ministry model has its flaws, the freedom to follow God's call within the life of the church has allowed us to enjoy our ministries more fully, to be more productive, and to have a greater sense of belonging to a caring and supportive community.

Questions for Reflection

1. How do your congregation's teams or committees structure their time? What percentage of time is devoted to business, to intentional relationship building, and to prayer and worship? If more time is needed for the latter two, what are ways of achieving this?
2. Do most of your congregation's teams or committees have narrowly focused responsibilities? What committees or teams seem to be overloaded? Which one is a good candidates for a ministry-team pilot test?

3. Imagine how a call-based approach to forming ministry teams, as described in this chapter, would work in your congregation, if you aren't currently organized this way. It's inevitable that some tasks will not get done and that people will experience that as a loss or as "wrong." What might you say when people complain or when people grieve the loss of a particular practice or program? How can you prepare people for the new reality?

CHAPTER 6

The Ministry of the Laity

When I arrived at UCC Norwell, the congregation was preparing to move to a ministry team model of organizing the congregation, which grew out of the congregation's understanding that all the people of UCC Norwell were ministers. The effectiveness of this model depended on individuals considering their call to ministry through the congregation *and* in the wider world.

Ministers to the World

For most of the life of UCC Norwell, our Sunday bulletin has echoed a conviction shared by many churches but actively and concretely pursued by very few: that the pastor and staff are the ministers to the congregation and the congregation is the minister to the world. For most churches, this is nothing more than a sentimental reminder toward that which all Christians should aspire. What I found upon my arrival in Norwell, however, was a congregation that was truly committed to this concept. The man who ran an operation that made vacuum pumps for assembly lines, the

woman who worked in human resources at a local bank, the man
who created a company that makes fiberglass compounds used in
the energy industry all referred to themselves as ministers. I was
blown away. This understanding of an individual's secular vocation
serving as a location and an opportunity for ministry was not held
by every single member of the community, but I was surprised by
how widespread the belief was that the goal of the Christian life
was to be a minister to the world.

If I doubted the conviction of the congregation on this point,
the leadership team that governed the church made it clear to me:
Our primary job was to help people understand that their whole
lives are opportunities for ministry. A parent is a minister. A clean-
ing person is a minister. An insurance salesperson is a minister.
Not only that, the belief at UCC Norwell was that God cares deeply
about the institutions that people work in. This was radical thinking that I needed to grapple with. The church I had been called
to serve wanted to make it clear to me that my job wasn't to get
people to do the work of the church, but rather to get people to
do the work of faith out in the world. I could have easily written
this concept off as nothing more than well-intentioned sentiment
worthy of placement in a worship bulletin—a neat idea no one had
to take too seriously. What I found, however, was a congregation
that was serious about putting their faith into action in their daily
lives. Their vocational settings were supposed to be their primary
location for doing ministry. This was not understood as an opportunity for a proselytizing ministry but rather a ministry of caring
and prophetic witness that could transform institutions and the
people who worked in them to powerfully promote justice, equal-
ity, and peace in the world. It was a wildly exciting and ambitious
goal, and one the church was clearly committed to pursuing. Little
did I know that encouraging people to do ministry in their workplaces would mean radically adjusting my understanding of how
work would get done within the church.

⚜ ⚜

Having my congregation tell me, in a variety of ways, that what I do in my daily work is important to the Church and of supreme importance to God, is life-changing! I now see everything I do through new eyes. How I worship, what I study, who I share with in small groups, how I manage my time, how I use my resources: everything becomes transformed. I am both challenged to look at my life and my commitments in a new way and to understand the Gospel in ever-broadening terms.

This understanding also, strangely enough, deepens my commitment to my local congregation. It helps me know why our gathered life as a community of faith is essential and life-giving. In addition to changing the way I look at my workplace and its impact on the world around me, it has changed the way I look at my congregation. Instead of the church being one more competing claim on my time, energy, and resources, it now stands at the center of my life, shaping the way I work and the way I see the world.

I know we have a ways to go to make this visibly true for everyone. But I believe we are on a profoundly important journey of recovering the whole ministry of the Church on behalf of the whole world.

Dick Broholm, former executive director, Center for the Ministry of the Laity, Andover Newton Theological School and former moderator at UCC Norwell

⚜ ⚜

CALL TO MINISTRY

Throughout the Bible, people are invited to take important steps of faith that we at UCC Norwell have come to refer to as *call*. Call is the process whereby the divine voice speaks to our mortal lives in ways that propel us forward in faith. In the Old Testament, God continually called people to go forth into new experiences, new lands, and new relationships. In the New Testament, Jesus's call to those he encountered was to literally follow in his footsteps. We at UCC Norwell believe that God calls to each and every one of us to invest our unique giftedness in the world in ways that serve to benefit all creation. When we look at biblical images of call, we can begin to develop a sense that an individual's *call* is always toward some sort of singular and grand purpose. The character of Noah was called by God to build the ark, just as the character of Jonah was called by God to go to Nineveh. Abraham was called to leave his family and his homeland to journey to a new and faraway land that his descendants would one day claim as their own. Moses was called to go to Pharaoh and demand the release of all Hebrew slaves so that they could begin their trek to the Promised Land. Ruth felt called to remain with Naomi as she made her way back to her homeland. David felt called to step out onto the battlefield with Goliath. Solomon felt called to build the first Temple in Jerusalem. Mary was called to bear the Son of God. John the Baptist was called to preach about the coming of the Messiah. Jesus was called to preach that the kingdom of God was at hand. And Paul was called to share the good news of Jesus Christ with the entire Gentile world.

Given this biblical perspective of call, it would be easy to assume that God's call on our lives is always meteoric and intensely focused. However, in UCC Norwell's experience, call is more often like watching fireflies at night. Call may be like a flash of light held for a moment against the darkest of backgrounds. In that moment God says, "You could go there, and I will be with you." Another light bursts into the darkness divinely promising, "You could go there, and I will be with you." Again, a small light flickers in the night, "And you could go there, and I will be with you."

With so many opportunities to offer service in the name of Jesus, and given the very real possibility that God's call is not unidirectional, the need for discernment when exploring one's call is all the more essential. We have come to believe that call is best discerned within community. Without other people of faith to help us focus, our pursuit of God's call might indeed be like a child trying to catch fireflies at night who changes direction every few seconds to follow the next burst of light they see. Discernment within Christian community can help us to focus on one of those pulses of light at a time, and it can encourage us to doggedly follow that illumination until our hands successfully clasp around our target.

GIFTS AND CALL FOCUS

A number of years ago, after thoroughly revamping our church's organizational structure, we decided to redefine the central mission and calling of our church. We had been so immersed in designing our new team-based model of ministry that we lost a bit of our sense of purpose and vision. We had been looking so hard at our structure, we failed to keep our eyes trained on our core business—calling people to ministry in their daily lives. Through a fairly exhaustive discernment process, our church council further established the mission focus of our church. We more firmly committed ourselves to helping individual members of our church discern their gifts and calling for ministry. When an individual truly understands their unique giftedness, and when they are able to discern where the Holy Spirit is calling them to invest those gifts in the world, that is when ministry begins. While the desire to help people understand their whole lives as ministry is a commitment our church has maintained almost from our community's inception, only over the past few years have we made gift and call identification the central focus of our congregation's life.

We have come to understand that the target we are pursuing as a congregation is actually an equation. The equation is a simple one, and certainly open to debate, but for us it has been helpful and clarifying: Gifts + Call = Ministry. Because we believe a Christian minister is a follower of Jesus Christ who invests his or her life and

his or her gifts in service to others for the glory of God, the goal of
the church is not to get more people to church on Sunday, or to increase enrollment in Christian education, or even to have greater
involvement in outreach ministries to the poor—the primary mission of the church is to help people understand that their entire life
is an opportunity for ministry.

All people are endowed by God with unique gifts and abilities
that are intended to be used for the good of all creation, and therefore every member of our community has special talents that God
wishes to be used to the fullest potential. And so the congregation's
role is to help people claim, and often reclaim, their sense of giftedness. The apostle Paul is clear in his Corinthian correspondence
that we are all gifted in different ways by the Holy Spirit, and the
gifts we have been given are to be used for the common good.

> Now there are varieties of gifts, but the same Spirit; and there are
> varieties of services, but the same Lord; and there are varieties
> of activities, but it is the same God who activates all of them in
> everyone. To each is given the manifestation of the Spirit for the
> common good. To one is given through the Spirit the utterance
> of wisdom, and to another the utterance of knowledge accord-
> ing to the same Spirit, to another faith by the same Spirit, to
> another gifts of healing by the one Spirit, to another the working
> of miracles, to another prophecy, to another the discernment
> of spirits, to another various kinds of tongues, to another the
> interpretation of tongues. All these are activated by one and the
> same Spirit, who allots to each one individually just as the Spirit
> chooses.
>
> 1 Corinthians 12:4–11

If we take time and really look, the number and diversity of gifts in
a single congregation is mind-boggling. There are poets and artists
and negotiators and cooks and teachers and caregivers and prayer
warriors and financial gurus and management specialists. There
are people with a capacity for deep wisdom, and others who are

wonderfully playful, and still others who are powerfully in touch with the Spirit of God. There are people with the gift of empathy, and people with the gift of vision, and people with the gift of leadership. I have been blown away by the multiplicity of gifts within the church community I serve as pastor. What is most surprising, however, is how unaware most people are about what they are truly good at. There is something about life—and our working lives in particular—that tends to grind out our sense of giftedness.

We at UCC Norwell have found that even in the best employment settings, the high expectations and critical nature of American work life tends to break people down instead of building them up. Also, as people make decisions about particular directions they want to go in life, those choices require them to invest some of their gifts while setting others aside. As we make our way through life, we often forget about gifts and passions that used to be very important to us, because we entered a career or an employment arena where they were not needed or utilized. Unfortunately, many people are employed in areas for which their gifts sets do not match the expectations and tasks that they are responsible to meet and accomplish. When a person's gifts and their vocational setting do not intersect well with one another, work life can be frustrating at best and downright demoralizing at worst. For the church to be vital and exciting, and for church members' lives to be enlivened and enriched, the church of Jesus Christ has to be a place where gifts, talents, interests, and abilities are discovered, affirmed, and used to the glory of God. We have come to realize that gift identification is the first step in helping a person understand his or her call to ministry.

DISCERNMENT AND DEPENDABLE STRENGTHS

If ministry was the goal toward which we were aiming, then we needed a comprehensive program for discerning both gifts and callings. For beliefs to be well grounded and flourish, they need to be supported by practices. We needed programs, processes, and practices that would help people understand their gifts and help them to discern their call to ministry. For the past several years our gifts and call ministry team has developed and implemented processes for individual and group discernment that help people gain a better sense of direction in their lives.

It began with an individual discernment process for people in vocational crisis or transition. Drawing on past accomplishments that gave a deep sense of joy, a member of our community who is in transition will share his or her history with a group of several individuals gathered around. These individuals will listen for gifts that are revealed through the personal story being told. After the conclusion of the narrative portion of the discernment process, the individual in discernment sits silently and listens as the group identifies a "hierarchy of giftedness" that highlights those abilities that are most pronounced in the narrative. This prioritization of gifts is then tested by the experiences and reflections of the individual in discernment—does it align with the individual's life and vocational experience? After agreement is reached about the general giftedness of the individual, the folks gathered begin to vocationally dream for the individual based on the gifts that were revealed. In a span of an hour or so, the group will generate dozen of imaginative vocational opportunities for the person in discernment to consider pursuing. Some of these ideas are wild and surprisingly liberating, while others are quite concrete and well-grounded. The individual in discernment then carefully reviews the list of ideas and selects three that are particularly interesting to him or her. Next, the group identifies resources that are available for the individual in order to pursue the ideas selected. (The foundation for this discernment process is from the work of Dr. Bernard Haldane, founder of Bernard Haldane Associates, a national career-consulting firm, currently the Center for Dependable Strengths, Olympia, Washington.[1] The process itself was brought to UCC Norwell by Dick Broholm, a longtime church member.)

At the end of a discernment session two things almost always happen for the individual in discernment. First, he or she is reminded of his or her talents. As mentioned earlier, we have found that there is something about work environments—even in the healthiest of settings—that tends to grind out our sense of giftedness. It is also true that when we make choices in our vocation life, we often have to set aside certain passions in order to pursue others. Sometimes we set aside something quite essential and then over time we forget about it entirely. I love when a discernment process helps a person recapture a gift or passion that they had long forgotten.

The other significant outcome of an individual discernment process is that the dreaming portion of the process always yields several concrete vocational opportunities that can be followed up on immediately. The people who go through this process always leave feeling affirmed, with a renewed sense of direction, increased optimism, and confidence. Over the years, people have made some radical career adjustments, others have stayed in a similar field but transitioned to a different employer, still others have been able to reimagine their role at their place of current employment in ways that allowed them to embrace their work with new life and excitement. These have become some of the most holy moments in the life of our congregation. Christ's people coming together to help discern God's call on the lives of church members, where extraordinary clarity is often achieved.

❧ ❧

I was apprehensive. A group of several folks from our community had gathered at the church a little before 9:00 a.m. on a Saturday morning to participate in a four-hour discernment process intent on uncovering my main gifts, talents, and interests. This would be followed by a right-brained activity that would explore possible avenues I might take, based on my gifts, which could lead me towards my "call" in life.

I had prepared for this day by reflecting on my entire life, going back as far as I could remember, listing my accomplishments— big and small, personal and professional, that had given me a deep sense of joy. I had then narrowed the list to ten accomplishments that I valued the most. Finally I had prepared myself to discuss these ten accomplishments in detail so the people could understand what I personally had done in order for them to discover and name my unique gifts, talents, and interests.

The reason I was having this discernment process was that I had been told by my boss that as a result of the Polaroid Corporation being in bankruptcy and in a restructuring process, my job was no longer required and I would be leaving in three months. Before I had actually left, I had been given a reprieve and had been offered another job within Polaroid that I felt was perfect for me; however, my future there was still quite precarious.

At UCC Norwell, we had begun to use a process based on the research and theory of Bernard Haldane, founder of a nationwide executive placement firm. His insight was to see people's joy-filled and energy-giving accomplishments as a clue to the particular gifts and strengths they would bring to any future endeavor. I believe that these abilities are a person's God-given gifts and strengths.

I must say I had reluctantly agreed to the process with a sense of uncertainty. We rarely think about our accomplishments, and rarer still, do we pull a group together to discuss those achievements in detail. However, I was facing the possibility of a major transition in my life and needed all the help I could get.

I was anxious as I started explaining my joys and accomplishments through specific stories; however, I soon relaxed and actually enjoyed remembering and talking about times in my life that held significant importance for me. After I finished, the group then proceeded to name my gifts one by one, and the facilitator of the discernment process listed them on a large flip chart. The group then did a weighted vote, which determined my top gifts. It was a humbling experience for me to reflect on the list of gifts, some of which I never would have named on my own, and to further recognize that every one of us has God-given gifts that make us unique.

The process continued, with the group suggesting a long list of employment possibilities I might consider based on their knowledge of me, my gift set, and my particular interests. One of the suggestions actually made a shiver go down my spine. I had thought I would have to leave Polaroid. The suggestion, though, was for me to stay there. "I wish Jerry could choose when he wanted to retire from Polaroid, staying in management with a self-motivated staff, wrapping up his career successfully and in his own time and under his own terms." I had not been able to name this; however, I definitely felt called to this course of action when I heard the words spoken.

The job I had been asked to do at Polaroid proved to be one where I could use my gifts to their fullest, and I left there four years later at exactly the best time for me and the best time for Polaroid.

Jerry Thornell, financial administrator and Gifts and Call Coordinator, UCC Norwell, and former financial manager, Polaroid Corporation

꙳ ꙳

This "Gifts and Call" process proved to be so life-renewing for people that we began to think of other ways to deliver the process to more members of our community. We began working with Luther Seminary in St. Paul, Minnesota, which trained and accredited some of our church members as facilitators to offer their Dependable Strengths workshop to larger gatherings of up to 24 members at a time.[2] The process includes theory, small-group participation, personal reflection, sharing of past "good experiences," and helping others. We believed that if people understood their personal strengths and gifts, they would be able to make more informed decisions about the work and ministry they were called to engage in.

Participants found it to be both a positive and affirming experience. Because the process had been so effective with adults, we began to develop a program for youth, using Luther Seminary materials as a base, so that our teenagers would know themselves better as they entered college or the workforce, and perhaps they would make better academic and social choices as they began to make their way in life on their own. This process uses small-group sharing and discernment along with personal reflection, and helps participants identify individual strengths, build self-esteem, and discern a greater sense of God's intent and purpose in their lives and in the lives of others.

When churches have contacted us to better understand how we are doing some of the creative ministerial work we are engaged in, they are initially most interested in our ministry team model. We assume this is because it is often in the organizational structure of a church that a community experiences the most stress. However, as we begin to talk with a faith community, they become increasingly interested in our gifts and call focus. The problem is that churches that have structural issues assume a gifts and call approach to ministry is an avenue for identifying people who can serve on depleted church boards and committees. It may be possible to use such an approach for cultivating leadership within the church, but we believe that the focus should be to help equip people for ministry in their daily lives. If a church focuses first on its mission and ministry outside the walls of the community— if the church truly becomes a life-giving force in people's lives— then folks begin to self-select for leadership within the church. Remember the ministry of the laity outside the church, and the laity will remember to participate in the ministries within the church.

SAYING NO TO THE CHURCH

If congregations are really going to encourage people to understand that their work lives are their primary opportunity for ministry, and if the church is going to affirm an individual's need to devote time and energy to that ministry, then people often need to be encouraged to say no to work in the congregation. While I immediately understood this consequence, the implementation took more faith than I suspect I had when I first arrived in Norwell. As one might expect, the people who truly understood the importance of the ministry of the laity outside the church were the people most active inside the church. As is the case in so many churches, the people who do the work in the congregation were doing *a lot* of work in the congregation. When I arrived in Norwell, a core group of members were serving on multiple boards and committees, and there was a sense that if anyone stepped back from leadership, important ministries would begin to fall apart. If that were truly the case, the idea of liberating certain members from their church work so they could focus on their ministry out in the world seemed to be a serious risk. However, if I was to attempt to live out the model of ministry I had been called to, and if I was going to start surrendering my agenda so that the Spirit could begin to have its way with the congregation, then encouraging people to say no to the church was a risk that needed to be taken.

The first couple of years of ministry in Norwell were marked by conversations that regularly encouraged people to step back from their church leadership commitments. If a mother already had her hands full with her children and was expecting another baby in the coming months, it was clear she needed to be encouraged to pull back from the Christian education team so that she could tend to her parental ministry at home. When the owner of a small business was struggling through a difficult personnel crisis at his firm, it was clear he needed to be freed up from his role on the board of trustees so that he could tend to his people at work. When a CPA in the church had his partner leave just prior to tax season, it was clear he had to be encouraged to step down from being a deacon so that he could faithfully serve his clients. Initially encouraging people to say no to congregational involvement seemed very risky; however, this practice had a couple of surprising by-products. First, other people began to step up. For whatever reason, the people doing all the work in the church didn't believe there were people in the wings ready to step into their ministries, and the people in the wings didn't think there was room for them on boards and committees that never seemed to transition leadership. Second, and perhaps most important, when an individual's work crisis abated, having been encouraged to say no to the church, they often wound up returning to the tasks of the community with a renewed sense of gratitude and energy.

This ethic of saying no has become a way of life for us now when we are nominating individuals for leadership positions within the church. Long gone are the days when a member of the nominating committee called someone up and begged them to join a board or team "because we can't find anyone else." When we need to fill a leadership role in the church today, after much prayer and discernment, we approach the person we want to have consider the role and tell him or her about the gifts we see he or she possesses that meet the needs of the position we want him or her to consider filling. After affirming the individual's gifts, he or she will be told, "While we would love to have you in leadership we realize that the time might not be right for you, there might be other more pressing ministries you are currently engaged in, so we really want to encourage you to say 'no' to us if you don't feel called at this time." That has become our genuine sentiment. We would rather have someone say no to the church if that means he or she can say yes to the ministry God is calling him or her to outside our community. Since adopting this practice, we have never been at a loss for leadership. I can't fully explain it, but by encouraging people to do God's work in the world, God has always provided us with enough people to do the work of the congregation.

RECEIVING A CALL TO THE CONGREGATION

Of course, we still need plenty of people to support the internal programs and ministries of the congregation. Without the laity working *in* the congregation, we wouldn't have a community that encourages people to minister *outside* the congregation. In a spirit of full disclosure, there have even been times when we have had to ask someone to make the congregation their priority when they probably didn't feel they had the time or talent for what they were being asked to do. In the life of the congregation, there are particular challenges and significant opportunities that often require a specific style of leadership and a certain leader. Over the past decade, we have restructured the organization of the church, restructured our staffing model twice, gone through two extensive visioning processes, engaged in major capital campaign conversations, dealt with an unexpected financial crisis, and there have been times when our leadership team and I have had to press someone to consider a call to leadership.

Developing a call-based leadership model can be quite liberating for people who have felt forced to do a whole host of church tasks they never wanted to do. However, the pendulum can swing so far in the other direction that people begin to equate call with "whatever I like doing." In the Bible, a call often comes at very challenging moments, and to people who feel completely unable to carry out the tasks they have been assigned. When there is a challenging task that needs to be done, and when we at UCC Norwell have identified the person we believe has the gifts for the tasks at hand, we will press quite hard for the person to consider stepping up to the challenge. While I still encourage people to say no if they really don't feel called to the ministry we are seeking them for, I will say flat out, "We need you to seriously consider this job. We know you are busy, we know you don't have much time for this, we know you have done lots of work for the church in the past, but we really need you now. We will absolutely understand if you have to say 'no' but we really need you to consider saying 'yes.'" Interestingly, since we have so confidently released church members from different obligations over the years, when we have to make a hard sell to a church member, they normally respond gladly and energetically. There are times in the church when we just have to press hard to get the leadership we need.

NEEDING AND AFFIRMING EXPERTISE

I am reminded of what I believed at the time to be some very wise counsel that I received while I was in seminary. A very fine Christian education professor made the point that you don't want to ask all the schoolteachers in your congregation to teach church school. Likewise, you don't always want to ask church members who work in the trades to be on the trustee board. This advice seemed prophetic to me. What if the woman who teaches second graders all year long really enjoys the financial markets and would love to work with the church endowment? What if the general contractor who deals with buildings all day long would really like to serve communion on Sunday mornings as a deacon? What if the banker in the congregation has a real passion and love for working with teenagers—are we going to push her to the finance committee?

I spent a good deal of time during my early years in Norwell really thinking creatively about where people might be called in the life of the church. I loved the idea that someone's ministry in the church could be remarkably life-giving if it is quite different from his or her ministry out in the world. It seemed to me that the church should be a place where an individual could have the opportunity to live out other aspects of his or her call as a Christian. While I still am fond of that ideal, I have come to know that as a congregation grows in size and complexity, it is quite helpful to have certain expertise in your leadership structure. When there is a staffing conflict, you want some people with solid human resources experience on your human resources team. When the boiler blows, the roof begins to leak, or the oil tanks need to be removed, you want some skilled tradesmen among your trustees. When you suddenly need to deal with a complicated financial matter, you want some strong financial expertise on your finance team.

The truth is, you need to find a balance. Lay members of your congregation who have passions and gifts that fall outside their traditional vocational roles should be allowed to creatively explore their call within the congregation. And when the congregation is in need of certain expertise, leaders should feel comfortable asking for what is needed.

Needing Education

At UCC Norwell we realized early on that for people to claim any part of their life as ministry, they first needed to understand their faith. Before you can be a minister you have to be a disciple. Learning the gospel naturally precedes living the gospel. The first disciples who gathered around Jesus engaged in an extensive learning and training program before Jesus sent them out into the world two by two to preach, teach, and cast out demons.

One aspect of our ministry that was clearly lacking in our early years together was an emphasis on adult Christian education. At 10:00 a.m. every Sunday morning, we would tell our people that they were ministers to the world; however, we would give them precious little training to prepare them for that role. This acknowledgment that education needed to be a central focus of our life together was slow to come, and we still struggle to craft discipleship programs that empower people to ministry; however, we are making important progress toward our goals. Later in this book I will describe our transition to an educational model where church school is offered to everyone, but here it is important to note that early on our model for ministry was handicapping our call to ministry. Like so many mainline Protestant churches, we had unwittingly created a dynamic on Sunday mornings that implicitly stated that learning was for children and worship was for adults. By having worship and church school at the same time, we were making a statement that adults didn't have to learn about their faith, and children didn't have to learn how to worship. This deficiency became ever more glaring until we finally got serious about addressing it. If churches are serious about empowering their people to ministry, then those same churches must be equally committed to helping their people learn about the faith they have been called to practice out in the world.

Another important realization helped shape our efforts to empower laity to ministry. Perhaps this is the case in all regions of our country, but New England is filled with historic churches that are quite sparsely attended on Sunday mornings. Our towns are filled with picturesque church buildings that are largely empty inside. When a new individual or family makes their way into one of these communities, the members of those churches descend upon them like a pack of ravenous wolves. So hungry for new members to fill an old and weary organizational structure, they might offer new visitors a seat on the deacon board at coffee hour on their first Sunday at the church. This might be an exaggeration, but I have heard so many "church shoppers" tell me stories about how on their first visit to a church they were told how much the church needed them, and how great it would be to have them on a board or committee. Needless to say, desperation is not a selling point for most people. While UCC Norwell wasn't in the habit of pouncing on new folks who visited our community, the truth is that when a new person wanted to get involved in the life of our church, his or her only avenue to such involvement was to join a board or committee. So if you were new to our community, the best way to fit in was to do some church work. Again, that seemed woefully inadequate and inappropriate.

When someone enters a community of faith, the first offer of involvement should not be to a task, but to a learning opportunity. Before people are invited to do the work of the church, they should be given ample opportunity to work on their faith. In fact, some of our most faithful and dynamic church leaders have stepped into leadership positions only after spending a considerable amount of time in Bible study or other educational offerings. This may sound very basic, and perhaps our church is the only community that got into this kind of rut, but we have found that if the laity are going to be empowered to think of themselves as ministers, then as a church we must give them plenty of opportunities to become disciples.

As a community of faith, we have come to understand that offering regular Bible studies, programs on gift and call discernment, book studies, and basic courses on Christian formation and faith practices are essential to the life and vitality of our congregation.

WORKPLACE VISITS

Workplace visits by the pastor to church members' places of employment are another expression of UCC Norwell's central focus on ministry of the laity.

Early on in my tenure at Norwell, a church leader suggested that I take some time to make visits to the workplaces of members of the congregation. Needless to say, this was not an idea that had been suggested during my seminary training. What would I do in someone's workplace? What questions would I ask? How would I even explain to people why I wanted to visit them where they worked? Thanks to some very thoughtful mentoring by leaders of the congregation who were passionately committed to workplace ministry, I found my way into this new kind of visitation ministry.

I began by asking people if I could visit them in their workplaces because it would give me insight into where they spent the majority of their lives.

It is true that you really don't know people until you know what they do for a living. When I would arrive at a place of work, it was always interesting to hear how I was introduced to others by the church member I was visiting. Some would unabashedly refer to me as their pastor, others would call me their friend, and often I would just be introduced by name instead of by the relationship we maintained. Over the years I have visited hundreds of workplaces—investment houses, transmission shops, law offices, bus companies, waste companies, oil companies, construction companies, schools, animal hospitals, restaurants, fire stations, banks. The list goes on and on. I typically schedule visits just before lunch so that I can get a tour of the workplace and an overview of the job being done, and then we will go out to lunch where I can more pointedly talk to the individual about how he or she either does or does not understand his or her vocational setting as a place of ministry. While certain jobs seem more exciting than others to me, I am always intrigued by the different work people engage in.

The benefits from this practice are far ranging. First, because of these visits, every Sunday morning I look out on my congregation and I know where folks have been all week. I have an image in my mind of what they have been doing. I have a new appreciation for how the word of God might apply to their lives. Second, by visiting their place of work I affirm what our church says we believe—that Christ and the church care about their vocation. And third, we get to talk directly about how what they do is ministry. It has gotten to the point where I can almost always find an angle of ministerial opportunity, even when the person working in the job can't see it themselves.

It is also an opportunity for the power dynamic to shift in the pastor/parishioner relationship. When the pastor is on someone's vocational turf, the church member becomes the authority and the pastor becomes the learner, and that exchange of roles can be mutually beneficial. I am amazed by what I have learned from spending time in factories, classrooms, and office buildings.

Of all the pastoral practices I engage in, workplace visits are among the most important and prophetic. If we as communities of faith say we believe that a workplace is a setting for ministry, then pastors and churches need to find creative ways to encourage that ministry.

HOLDING IN TRUST

If we truly believe that ministry is primarily done in people's daily lives, and if God does really care about the institutions that employ us, then the church community should play an active role in supporting church members and the organizations they work in when those members and organizations encounter challenges. While this is still a growing edge for our community, on a number of occasions we have gathered people of faith around a church member who is struggling with important organizational decisions. Six to eight people, with the guidance of a trained facilitator, gather to support an individual member in the workplace ministry. When a business leader is struggling to know how to faithfully downsize his or her company, when a health-care professional is wrestling with how to cope with a broken health-care system, or when an entrepreneur is dealing with staffing issues, church members have been called together to pray, listen, discern, and brainstorm a way forward.

On a practical level, I am never entirely sure if this effort of holding a church member and his or her organization in trust helps to resolve the issues that are being faced. I am certain, however, that the practice of surrounding a member of our community with prayer, support, and careful suggestions further helps people understand that faith and vocation go hand in hand. If Christian communities care about the institutions people work for and the challenges those vocational settings present, then perhaps everyone can begin to believe that God cares too. We have come to believe that for church to be relevant in the world and vibrant in its own communal life, communities of faith need to make a serious commitment to be involved in the many different settings in which their people have an opportunity for ministry.

THEOLOGY OF INSTITUTIONS

More recently, we have been experimenting with using an adapted version of our individual gifts and call discernment process to help entire churches and other institutions discover their call to ministry. We believe that God not only cares for individual people and communities of faith around the globe, but that God also cares deeply about the institutions we serve. Institutions wield significant power and authority. They can be a force for good and a source of inspiration. In their own way they have souls and missions just like individuals. Institutions, like human beings, can become sick, they can deviate from their intended course, and there are times when they can be either complicit in sinful behavior or instigate it all together. There is a natural and deep human draw to form institutional bonds that serve to protect and preserve our way of life. If human beings are created in something like God's image, and if God loves us as children, then God must also have affection for the divine image as it is revealed in the assembled organizations we participate in.

Too often we think of corporations, governmental agencies, and health-care conglomerates as soulless entities that aim to take advantage of people and do harm to the common good. While there are, and have been, institutions that have been injurious in shocking ways, there are many more businesses that strive to make genuine and life-giving contributions to the world. As a sinful and often suspect institution itself, the church should be in the business of calling institutions to account when they are acting unjustly, while at the same time encouraging and celebrating the remarkable work that institutions both perform and preserve. If institutions are places where so many of our people are called to invest their gifts and engage in ministry, then it is safe to assume that God cares deeply about the success and well-being of those organizations. In fact, if Gifts + Call = Ministry is true for individuals, then perhaps that same equation can be used for institutions. That might be particularly true for churches that wish to discern where they might be called to serve the world. In the end, God loves us and the organizations into which we invest our lives.

We began asking ourselves if we could fashion the process so that it could work for an institution, particularly the church. Instead of engaging in what might often seem to be a daunting visioning process, could a church community simply discern its unique giftedness, and where it is called to invest those gifts in the future?

We suspect that identifying a community's unique giftedness, and then discerning where Christ might be calling that community to invest those gifts in the world, might just be a more gentle and faithful way for a church to find direction. This process had us look at our history over the years to identify those major events, happenings, and achievements that we were proud of. Using these as a base, we then developed gifts and traits that the church had demonstrated over the years. We also surveyed the entire congregation to get up-to-date information about our gifts and traits, and we studied current secular and theological trends that would be affecting us. We then convened two groups of twelve people who, using all of the data collected, discerned what areas needed to be points of focus and generated some significant suggestions and ideas about the congregation's current call to ministry. The final step was to summarize the data and the ideas and to roll out the information using small meeting formats to inform the congregation and to also get feedback and reflections.

This is certainly a scattering seeds moment for this mission that is so important to our church. We know we have a rich and exciting discernment program in hand, and we are actively seeding it in different relational environments to see what takes root and grows. We know that some of our efforts will not meet with the success we hope, but we trust that if we keep planting the idea that Gifts + Call = Ministry, somewhere we will witness a remarkable harvest.

Questions for Reflection

1. What practices does your congregation have in place that recognize and affirm the ministry of people "in the world"— in their workplaces, at home, in community service activities, in their places of recreation? What additional things could be done?

2. If your congregation uses a gifts discernment process with members, review it to evaluate whether it helps people consider both service within the congregation and their call to ministry in the world. If it doesn't, think about what might be added so that it reflects this balance.

3. If your congregation does not use a gifts discernment process with members, how are people invited to participate in congregational ministries and governance, and how well is this process working? What could be done to improve it?

4. Do you agree or disagree with the statement that "the pastor and staff are the ministers to the congregation and the congregation is the minister to the world," and why?

CHAPTER 7

The Ministry of the Pastor

At UCC Norwell, members are the ministers scattering seeds and tending growth as they respond to their calls to serve in and through the congregation and in the world. What, then, does their pastor do? Not long after arriving at Norwell, I came to the conclusion that my job involved waiting, watching, and witnessing the work of God in the world while tending to these ministers and the growth God provides. As pastor and people follow the agenda of Jesus Christ and the Spirit's leading, the ministry of the laity and of the pastor go hand in hand.

PREACHING AND COMPASSION: THE BREAD AND BUTTER

Just before I left seminary, I had a moment of anxiety, wondering if I had what it takes to be a pastor. I had a growing sense of the many and varied tasks I would be asked to perform, and I knew I wouldn't be gifted at all of them. Could it be possible that I would be overwhelmed by expectations I could not meet? It had happened to plenty of pastors over the years, so why not me? I shared my concern with my supervising pastor, and she offered me words of encouragement that have sustained me in ministry to this day. "Chapin, preach with excellence and love the people, and you will be just fine."

While I would never want to suggest that I have become a master homiletician any more than I would want to infer that I am somehow uniquely compassionate—striving to preach with excellence, and striving to love the people are, in fact, the bread and butter of the pastoral profession. If a pastor works hard to become an effective communicator of the gospel of Jesus Christ while he or she makes his or her best effort to embrace the people they are called to serve, all will be well. Whatever risks are taken, whatever new ministerial initiatives are put into action, whatever missteps are made along the way, when preaching and compassion are paramount, forgiveness among the people abounds because the heart of ministry has been faithfully sustained by the pastor. I cannot begin to count the many times this core conviction has kept me grounded when a thousand different concerns and anxieties seemed to assail me. Being part of a growing and vibrant church is a wonderful gift; however, church growth increases the demands on pastors, often pressing us into new missions and ministries for which we are not entirely prepared. Therefore, it is helpful to always keep before us the heart of our pastoral calling. Clarity of call can lead to vitality within our vocation. And in a church that grows in surprising and unexpected ways, being grounded with a strong base is all the more important.

Part of the Family

Loving the people sounds like an admirable and perhaps even idyllic goal, but as everyone knows, love is difficult and demanding work. However, it is essential work that must occur if a congregation is to thrive. The pursuit of love should be a primary focus within the life of a church, not just because the gospel commands it, but because trust is an invaluable component of love. Church growth and vitality invariably require some degree of risk taking, and to take risks, a congregation must trust one another. Love and trust go hand in hand. The more trust that exists between a pastor and the people he or she serves, the more daring the ministry a community can engage in.

As is true in all human relationships, it is nearly impossible to develop either love or trust among people who do not know one another. For too long, in my opinion, clergy have been encouraged to keep a professional distance between themselves and the members of their congregations. Friendships between pastors and parishioners are frowned upon. As a result, clergy tend to operate under the assumption that the people they serve should freely open up their entire lives to them, while the pastor, for his or her part, remains a bit emotionally and relationally removed from the people. This has always struck me as a missed opportunity as well as a practice that disregards so much of the teaching of the Bible. I cannot imagine Jesus or Paul imposing professional distance between themselves and the people they referred to not only as their friends but also as their family. Paul's letters, even the ones that are filled with anguish, are endowed with the deepest love and affection. Paul clearly shared his whole life with the people he served. To the Christians in Thessalonica, he wrote, "So deeply do we care for you that we are determined to share with you not only the gospel of God but also our own selves, because you have become very dear to us" (1 Thess. 2:8). Paul encouraged the leaders he worked with to do the same.

Perhaps one of the reasons that the ministerial creativity and daring of the early church is not witnessed in our communities is that the kind of love and trust so familiar to Jesus and the apostles is something we have come to view with suspicion. However, for the pastor and people who desire to break down the artificial barriers between one another, remarkable blessings await. When the Christian family is precisely that—a family—where love and affection and trust abound, the building blocks of church growth and vitality are at hand. I believe that closing down or setting arbitrary limits on the depth of sharing and caring between any portion of the membership of Christ's community serves as a hindrance to the Holy Spirit. Conversely, when pastors and the people they serve are open to one another, when they share authentically the joys and sorrows of life, when they stand before God as one people, that is when the Spirit can be set free in truly surprising and wonderful ways.

As pastors, to love the people means to know the people and to have the people know us in return. That knowledge can lead to a love and trust that can allow communities to engage in a whole range of daring ministries that can breathe new life and possibility into the most calcified of churches. I suspect that church growth and vitality are only possible when growth and vitality are allowed to flourish between individual members of the community— clergy being among that sacred membership!

GIVING PERMISSION

When people love one another, they surrender the need to control one another. When a pastor isn't spending time trying to gain control over the people, and when the membership of a community stops trying to control the clergy in their congregation, they often find themselves giving permission to one another in ways that affirm their respective ministries. Much has been written on the importance of churches being permission-giving institutions, and I can attest to the wisdom of this practice. As long as a ministerial initiative falls within the general scope of our church's mission, I almost always find myself enthusiastically encouraging parishioners to follow their sense of call. According to the parables we

looked at in chapter 3, seeds are scattered in many less than promising ways. If I don't know where seeds will fall, if I don't know
what kind of ground will be receptive to what is planted, if I don't
know where the harvest will be, why would I ever want to limit
the scope of the sowing? I don't need to be personally invested
or even particularly interested in every ministry initiative that is
sown in my church. I just need to be doggedly convicted that the
more seeds that are scattered, the more ministry will be able to take
root. Even in the most lay-empowered churches, pastors serve as
gatekeepers for the ministry of the church. It often only takes one
discouraging word from a pastor to scuttle the ministerial aspirations of a church member. Pastors should not serve as obstacles to
ministry. So, when a member of my community enters my office
and shares the seed of an idea for ministry that excites them, I do
all I can to get them to go out and plant it. I don't know if the initiative will grow to maturity or if the soil of the congregation is not
prepared to receive what is shared. Frankly, I don't care. I am not in
the control business, I am in the permission-giving business. If my
encouragement ends in a ministry that fails to take root, the love
and trust I have cultivated within our community will more than
compensate for the lack of success.

I have also found that by giving people permission to follow the Holy Spirit's leading within the congregation, that gift is
returned to me as well. Because I have made *yes* my default setting instead of *no*, I am extending that same encouragement by
the people I serve. If I want to take a risk in worship, if I want to
begin a new program within the community, if I want to teach a
class at a local seminary, if I need to leave work early on a Monday
afternoon to coach my child's basketball team, the answer is a re-
sounding yes. *Yes* is a wonderfully contagious word that can instill
life and vitality within a congregation, whereas *no* is almost always
a defeating word that can have a perilous effect on the hopes and
dreams of people of faith. Scattering seeds of ministry and faith is
encouraged.

There are, however, certainly times to set limits. There are situations when a well-timed *no* is the most essential word that can be said. And a *yes* should not be offered merely because of a fear of disappointing people. Neither word should be offered out of a sense of cowardice; to do so might be at the expense of the church's mission and moral responsibility. With that said, as a general rule, pastors and the people they labor with should be in the business of encouraging one another, granting one another permission to follow the Spirit's call on their lives, and releasing their respective desire to control what the Lord is trying to do in their midst.

COMFORTABLE WITH CHAOS

One of the consequences of giving permission for people to follow the call of the Spirit on their lives and on the life of the church is that as ministry begins to spring up all over the place, very few people—the pastor included—know all that is happening within the community. When you commit to blanketing the ground with seeds of gospel love and faith, you will often lose control of the outcome. Surrendering control is difficult enough for most people, but "not knowing" what is going on can give most people fits. At the United Church of Christ in Norwell, as multiple ministries began to be launched simultaneously, people would ask me about a particular program, or a specific meeting, or an upcoming event at the church and more often than not I wouldn't have much information to give them. To this day I do not know when the prayer shawl ministry team meets, I do not know who is on the health awareness ministry team, and I do not know what new service projects our mission and outreach ministry team will present us with this year.

I gladly admit that the "not knowing" was a bit unsettling at first. The difficulty wasn't so much that there were activities going on in the church that I didn't have a guiding hand in, but rather, it was unsettling to have people contact me only to get the impression that their pastor didn't know what was going on in the church. This twinge of self-consciousness passed after a while, because it had to—ministries were taking off and I soon lost the ability to keep track of them all. And if the truth be told, I didn't want to be involved in all the ministry of the church. It is an unspoken rule that a pastor should take an intense interest in all the ministries the church engages in. It may be an implied rule, but I do not know a single pastor who doesn't find themselves less interested and invested in some ministries than others. That is certainly true of the people in the church, so we might as well admit that it is true of pastors too. I fully affirm all the ministry going on in our church, and yet I am grateful I don't have to be a part of it all.

With people engaged in ministries beyond both my control and my interest, with an organizational structure that continues to expand, and with a focus on lay leadership that relies on already busy people doing even more work, a pastor has to learn to be comfortable with a degree of chaos. This is a bitter pill to swallow if you like order. Scattering seeds is not a helpful model for doing ministry if you are the type of person who just can't bear a little untidiness. It seems to be part of our human nature to try to bring order out of chaos. Personally, I prefer order, clarity, and definition in my life. And yet, while I appreciate the magnificence and symmetry of the gardens of Versailles, I find a different, but no less awe-inspiring beauty in a wildflower garden or in the way evergreens randomly mix with hardwoods in a New England forest. While it goes against my preferred nature, I have found beauty in chaos. And while I could never have imagined saying this in seminary, I wouldn't trade my wildflower garden in Norwell for the most finely manicured community of faith in the country.

SHELVING THE AGENDA

Scattering seeds as a method for cultivating church growth and vitality often means shelving your personal agenda as a pastor. If the Holy Spirit is going to move freely about pastors' communities, then pastors need to be willing to surrender much of their image of what a church should be. All pastors have ideas about what a community of faith should look like and what success within that community should look like. We come into churches with passionate convictions about our calling to help shape and guide the body of Christ. It can be quite alarming when that body begins to move under its own power and out of our control. When you want to move a community in a certain direction, and when the body of Christ moves as if it has a mind of its own, the frustration can be real. As I began to realize that the Holy Spirit was alive and well and moving within our community, I had to come to terms with the reality that much of the time my job was simply to get out of the way. There were plenty of times when I realized that my role and my image for ministry could have served as a hindrance to what the Lord was trying to do in our community. Stepping to the side and letting the Spirit blow right on past me has become an important part of my pastoral vocation.

That has meant, of course, that there have been many times in the life of the church when I haven't gotten my way. I think back on decisions around staffing or structure when I felt passionately convicted that I knew the best way forward, only to have the gathering of faithful people around me go in an entirely different direction. It is quite a challenge to spend most of your waking hours trying to address a particular issue in the church only to have the laity gather for a board and committee meeting, and, after an hour or two, decide on an entirely different course of action. Early on in my ministry at Norwell, I struggled with decisions that were made that went against my better judgment. It was particularly frustrating when a decision like that went badly. It was also distressing to see work done by laity that could have been done much more thoroughly if a trained staff member had been assigned to the task. However, through this sense of frustration emerged a critically important understanding of ministry that has continued to be a blessing to me.

Now I understand that church work isn't about getting the right answer any more than it is about doing a perfect job on a particular task. Everything we do is about building community. The church is primarily in the relationship business—at our best we try to cultivate relationships with God and with one another. Thoughtful communal discernment through which lay members of the congregation are not only listened to but also looked to as guiding lights is part of community building. Valuing dissenting opinions is part of community building. Frankly, making a poor decision together is preferable to making a perfect decision that breaks people apart. I would rather do a mediocre job on a particular task if it allows for community building than insist on my own way to the detriment of others. When a pastor forces his or her agenda on a congregation, even if that agenda is clearly the most sensible path ahead, that pastor can begin to break down the very community he or she was called to nurture and grow. Having come to the realization that all the work of the church was about building community, I found it much easier to shelve my own agenda because I had a Bible full of evidence that the Holy Spirit is a master community builder. All I needed to do was to encourage practices that provided avenues for the Holy Spirit to enter our community, and then trust that the important work of church growth and vitality would follow. As a pastor, the only real agenda I had to concern myself with was to make sure the people were engaging in faith practices that opened them to the movement of the Spirit. As long as I made sure the people received communion, devoted themselves to prayer, and took time to study the Scriptures, the rest of my agenda could be set aside and the Lord's agenda could move forward relatively unencumbered.

Letting Go without Giving Up

As this spirit of pastoral yielding began to take root in our congregation, furthered by our move toward a ministry team organization model, there were staff members who struggled to manage the transition. Our model for ministry relies significantly on individual members of the congregation feeling personally called to a particular task in the church. This was a liberating concept in the life of a congregation that was encumbered with far too many tasks it felt it *should* be doing. However, in the past, certain staff members took this ethic too far and used it as an excuse to give up on programs that did not garner much initial support. Letting go of our need to press a pastoral agenda does not mean giving up on the essential work of calling forth gifts from within Christ's community. Just because my agenda, or my image for ministry, or my vision for the church isn't the chosen path for the congregation doesn't mean I throw up my hands in frustration and give up. The ministry of the laity and the ministry of the pastor go hand in hand. Church programs are not hot potatoes tossed between equally reluctant parties.

The goal of the pastors and lay leaders of a congregation is to let go of their own agendas so that, together, pastor and people can begin to follow the agenda of Jesus Christ.

REMEMBERING THE MISSION

While I continue to be amazed at the way ministry can take root in a congregation if a pastor sets aside his or her need to micromanage the community, there is one peril of this kind of hands-off ministry approach that often catches me by surprise and bites me. If you decide to go with the flow of the Spirit in your congregation, you might find yourself suddenly asking, "What are we supposed to be doing here?" "What is our core business?" "What are we primarily about?" Each year, normally around our annual meeting, I find myself asking these questions. The seeming lack of focus of our ministry can prompt within me a desire to know if there is anything upon which we should be fixing our gaze. Do we have some core convictions that can serve as tethers as new ministries begin to bloom in their own time and in their own way? If I am willing to relinquish my desire to control the program life of my congregation, is there anything I should cling to? While our church is not a huge community, there is enough ministry going on that I begin to lose my place.

So, from time to time, I recognize that it is my pastoral responsibility to try to identify our central calling. I do this as much for myself as for the people I serve. Over the years this has meant the formulation of different statements or initiatives that have helped to clarify our communal calling. Our mission statement was one of my first attempts to gain some sense of congregational direction: "We are a Christ-centered community called to ministry." The following year we printed up new letterhead that was embossed with our vision for our gathered life: "Making Disciples, Equipping Ministers." There was another year when I challenged the leadership of our church to start thinking about giving up the title of *member* and taking on the title of *minister*. Because the transformation of members into people who understood their lives as ministry was a central calling in our community, I had visions of sending our denominational offices the number "0" when we were asked how many members we had in our church. If they called to ask where all our members had gone, we would let them know we don't have members anymore, but we have several hundred ministers. These efforts, however well or ill conceived, represent an ongoing pastoral role that can never be surrendered. Because churches and pastors lose focus quickly, often for the very good reason that a ton of really faithful and exciting work is getting done within the church, it is the pastor's role to help the people focus on our primary calling: to be followers of Jesus Christ and ministers to the world Christ loves.

In the midst of all the ministerial activity, someone has to remember and witness to the primary calling of Christ's church. The pastor has to be the standard bearer of that mission.

Church vitality is cultivated and supported by certain leadership characteristics. Here are some of the characteristics that I have witnessed in pastoral leadership here at UCC Norwell.

- There is excellence in preaching and teaching.
- They have the ability to get and keep everyone's attention and maintain the focus.
- Different than some leadership styles, we have found that it is best for there to be real bonds of friendship between pastor and laity. This may go against conventional wisdom and what is taught in seminary; however, we have seen that this friendship and vulnerability creates real connections, support, and trust.
- Their time is carefully managed. Staff responsibilities should be clear so nothing slips between the cracks. A pastor can be open to all; however, meetings and pastoral visits need to be carefully scheduled and adhered to. They need to look for balance and not overload themselves as crises will arise that will demand their time.
- Careful listening and honest feedback are key. There needs to be a true feeling that the pastor has a real concern for everyone.
- The congregation wants to love the pastor and his or her family and is allowed the freedom to do so, as is the pastor.
- Trusted advice, mentoring, and counsel are sought after and welcomed by the pastor. It is important to be sure they are hearing all viewpoints in order to make the best suggestions and decisions.
- Pastoral praying and asking others to pray deepens relationships and allows the Holy Spirit to work among us.
- They need to think big picture, with the ability not to just see their own vision, rather they help the congregation see their own vision and set their own paths.
- They demonstrate a sincere interest and respect for the financial affairs of the church. Talk openly and comfortably about stewardship and giving.

- They are able to identify and affirm the right leaders for various areas, dependent upon their gifts and interests, and let them take the responsibility.
- They demonstrate patience while providing leadership that moves the congregation forward, striving for results.
- Their integrity is above question.
- They show humility and hold others up when successes are recognized while standing tall and taking the heat when things fail.
- Their interest and focus includes all people in the congregation from the very young to the seniors.
- They demonstrate a life in balance. They ensure that family time is held sacred.
- Their ability to lead is by the pastor's own desire for personal growth, including advanced education, outside teaching opportunities, and outside leadership opportunities.
- And most importantly, they demonstrate a good-hearted sense of humor.

Jerry Thornell, financial administrator and
gifts and call coordinator, UCC Norwell, and
former financial manager, Polaroid Corporation

ENJOYING THE LIFE

Finally, I believe that the ministry of the pastor should be an absolute blast. Clergy are called to serve an organization that has been founded to share the good news of Jesus Christ, and I believe we should have a good time doing it. If a person is truly called to it, the pastoral life is a truly good life—a great life, in fact! There are costs involved in the pastoral life, to be sure, but the joy that comes from such service is, in my opinion, unequalled. That great life can be most fully enjoyed if a pastor is clear about what he or she is called to do, and what he or she is not called to do within the life of the congregation. I have found that the ministry of scattering seeds—not worrying where the seeds fall, or which seeds will mature—is a deeply liberating model of ministry for the pastor. A scattering seeds approach to ministry allows a pastor to realize the ultimate reality that he or she is not in control. It allows for an ethic of hard work without an overemphasis on arbitrary measures of success. Most importantly, pastors who decide that their work is to simply cover the ground with the word and ways of God can sleep soundly and peacefully at night knowing that the Spirit continues to work long after they have taken their hand off the plow. This model of ministry is thus affirmed in the morning when the pastor awakes and finds that seeds have begun to sprout and grow. I have seen it happen far too often to doubt it anymore. As the apostle Paul indicated, we may plant and water the seeds, but it is God who gives the growth. The joy of the pastoral life truly begins when clergy embrace that truth.

Questions for Reflection

1. If you are a pastor, think of a time or times when this statement was true for you: "Whatever risks are taken, whatever new ministerial initiatives are put into action, whatever missteps are made along the way, when preaching and compassion are paramount, forgiveness among the people abounds because the heart of ministry has been faithfully sustained by the pastor." What happened—what were the risks, initiatives, or missteps? How did communicating the gospel and your relationship with people make a difference?

2. As a pastor, lay leader, or congregational member, what are your expectations about the relationship between the pastor and congregational members? If you are in the "professional distance" camp, why is that? What benefits have you

seen? What are the down sides? If instead you prefer a close family-like dynamic, why is that? What benefits have you seen? What are the down sides?

3. As a leader, what experiences have you had in giving permission and giving up control, and then living with some chaos? Whose image of "what church should be" is guiding the congregation you serve?

4. Think of some examples of times in your congregation when the pastors and laypeople shared leadership and worked side by side to follow the agenda of Jesus Christ. Does it happen often, or is it rare?

5. "It is the pastor's role to help the people focus on our primary calling: to be followers of Jesus Christ and ministers to the world Christ loves." Does this statement sum up the pastor's role for you? If not, what would you add or change?

6. For pastors: Do you feel "the joy that comes from service" in your ministry, most of the time? If not, how might a scattering seeds approach make your ministry more joy-filled?

CHAPTER 8

Worship and Education for All

As mentioned previously, UCC Norwell discovered early on in our transition to ministry teams and our renewed emphasis on the ministry of the laity, that we must be equally committed to helping people learn about the faith they have been called to practice out in the world. Tending to growth, we believe, requires tending to worship and education for all ages.

A Broken Educational Model

Arguably the most significant shift in our congregation over the past decade has been our emphasis on education and worship for all. Like many mainline Protestant churches in our country, worship and church school for children were held at the same time. Parents and other adults worshiped upstairs while children attended church school downstairs. The children were invited to join in worship when there was a children's message, or when it was Youth Sunday. Even on the surface of this arrangement we recognized numerous flaws. First, and most immediately pressing, was that issue of recruiting church school teachers. Because church school was held during worship, and because worship was an engaging activity for adults, most adults avoided teaching because they didn't want to miss Sunday's service. We also found that when there was a behavioral issue with a child in church school that required parental involvement, it was fairly challenging to find a parent in the sanctuary during worship. There was also the significant issue of teacher education. We were offering a fairly paltry assortment of Christian education opportunities for adults, which meant that the only time that adults really learned anything about their faith was during worship. If teachers couldn't attend worship, that meant they were not learning themselves, and if they were not learning themselves, what were they prepared to teach our children? This was most glaringly apparent in the fact that our minister of children's education never had the opportunity to attend worship. While teachers taught only a few sessions at most during a given program year, our minister of children's education was downstairs in our basement classrooms all year long. In that educational model, the leading educator of our children never had the opportunity to worship or learn more about the Christian faith. We also noticed that once children completed our confirmation program, and their formal church school experience ended, they rarely if ever returned to the church on Sunday mornings. We created a system whereby eighth through twelfth graders went to youth programs on Sunday evenings, but only participated in worship on Easter, Christmas Eve, and Youth Sunday. A cursory examination of our educational program revealed that there were glaring issues, but what slowly came into greater focus was the implicit and unacceptable message we were giving to the members and friends of our congregation.

IMPLICIT MESSAGE

While we were slow to come to the realization, we began to understand that our educational model was sending an unintended, yet deeply unhelpful message to our congregation. Having adults worshiping God at the same time that our children were in church school communicated that Christian education for adults was not important and that having children participate in worship was not important to them or to our faith community. We had not intended to send such a careless message, but our church tradition and convention was communicating just that—children needed only education, and grown-ups needed only worship.

The fruits of this system were as disappointing as sour grapes. Biblical illiteracy in our adult population was rampant, and disinterest in worship from our children and young adults was endemic. Once we realized the unhealthy faith dynamic we were sustaining, we knew it had to change if we were going to grow in faith as a community. Due to teacher recruitment issues, over the years we had convened different task forces to look into other educational models we might employ. We came to the conclusion that our course ahead would involve more education and commitment on the part of church staff and membership. We knew that worship was more like an educational vitamin supplement than a full meal, and we knew that if children didn't learn to worship it was unlikely that they would ever acquire the taste for it. We began to suspect that expanding to a two-hour model for education and worship on Sunday morning was the path we needed to take. However, we were reluctant to break from our traditional model, largely, and personally, because of fear. Would people embrace a more significant commitment on Sunday mornings? Or would people leave the church because new educational demands were placed on them? I had this fearful vision that the church might break down with added demands on people's lives, and I might be the one responsible for its downfall. We knew our educational model was spiritually unhealthy and structurally compromised, and it was unclear if anyone had the courage and resolve to make a change that might fix it.

OPPORTUNITY IN CRISIS

Just as a number of our church leaders were coming to the realization that increased educational opportunities for everyone was a fight worth having, or perhaps, more accurately—a hill worth dying on—our church was jostled by an unexpected transition in pastoral leadership. A beloved pastor of our church, who had overseen many of our educational offerings, needed to relocate to England with her family. This presented us with some immediate questions about how we would support our educational programs.

While unexpected, church leadership transitions are part of the life of Christian communities, and they always present opportunities for growth and change. We quickly seized upon the leadership transition as a minor crisis that might afford us great opportunity. One of the great blessings of human relationships is that people tend to band together to do what needs to be done when unexpected or unfortunate life circumstances are encountered. The outpouring of goodwill and generosity in a crisis situation has a way of overcoming daunting challenges and obstacles, at least for a time. However, once the initial shock of a crisis or tragedy has abated, we tend to quickly revert back to our less-than-generous and less-than-creative way of living. So, while a transitional crisis can serve as an important opportunity for growth, that window of opportunity can shut as quickly as it opened. Swift and decisive action is often required in order to take advantage of transitional moments.

This is one of the few times when I took the ball and ran with it. With the encouragement of council, I drafted a proposal for a new approach to worship and education, and the church followed it. We used a moment of crisis to enhance our gathered life. Thankfully, church leadership recognized the importance of the situation we were in and acted to strengthen our educational ministries by enacting an initiative that offered education and worship for everyone. We would extend our Sunday morning offerings to allow for comprehensive adult education and worship participation for our children.

Since we did not have the pastoral support we were accustomed to after one of the pastors left, we also transitioned to an "All Church Meeting Night" when all our ministry teams meet for worship, fellowship, and to tend to issues of church operations. We began to quickly shift to a model where we intentionally gathered as a community. We were choosing to learn together, to worship together, and to conduct our business together. We implemented our transitional model for education, worship, and organizational structure at the beginning of our program year in 2006, and I braced myself for what I believed would be an aggressive push back and a significant fallout from our membership.

EDUCATION FOR ALL

The transition was surprisingly smooth at first, with some immediate and truly hopeful results. The opportunity to offer adult Christian education on Sunday mornings reinvigorated our adult Christian education ministry team, and within short order we were able to offer several different adult education classes every Sunday morning. Because of our limited offerings in previous years, this meant that participation by adults in Christian education hit levels we had never seen before. On any given Sunday, we would have dozens of adults gathering for Bible studies, book studies, and classes on spiritual disciplines and other topics. While the actual percentage of our congregation who participated in our "Church School for All Ages" was less than we had initially hoped, the rise in the overall numbers were dramatic. Not only that, it suddenly became much easier to recruit children's church school teachers because church school was no longer competing with Sunday worship for adult involvement. Without question, the number of young children in our program declined due to a lack of willingness by some parents to commit to an extra hour of church on Sunday morning. That said, with the addition of our middle school and high school Bible study classes, the participation of our teenagers on Sunday mornings ballooned. While we always long for a deeper commitment to education by more members of our congregation, we could not ignore the fact that the life and vitality of our church had been enhanced by increased time spent together in educational activities.

⁂

UCC has been my church since I attended youth group. After many years of schooling, I brought my family back to UCC. It wasn't long before I found myself a single mother of four. I work long hours and thus found myself struggling to find family activities that would bring us together. Early on I felt it was extremely important for my children to have exposure to faith and exposure to people seeking to become better people through their faith. UCC was the place.

Initially, the church service on Sundays consisted of an hour-long service in the sanctuary with church school for the kids downstairs. As I had four children in church school, I felt obligated to sign up to help out with church school. Church attendance at that time was quite a chore. Not only was I exhausted from my long week at work and my struggle to prepare four cranky, energetic children for attendance, but I also had to drum up the energy to attempt to play a mentoring or coaching role for a bunch of other children. On the days I was able to attend service, I felt that I was barely able to clear my head before it was over and I was rounding up my children.

When the transition to adult education offerings and church school preceding the worship service occurred, I felt excited to have an opportunity to learn with other adults, knowing that my children were undertaking a similar process. I was also apprehensive about spending the worship service together with my children as I envisioned the kids fighting with one another... the "he's looking at me cross-eyed" thing. But by the third week my excitement only grew and my apprehension lessened.

One of the first classes I took was one in which we investigated family traditions and how they impact our lives. This class helped me prioritize activities with my family. Dinnertime became my focus for connecting with my family during the week. There were book clubs, Islamic studies, Parenting in the Pew, and many others. I enjoyed them all. One of my favorites was, and is, Church School 101, in which the Bible passage from the sermon that Sunday is discussed. It is fascinating to hear all the different perspectives from one Bible verse.

Over the months, I came to realize that my hour of adult education helped me connect with many of the adults in the church community in new ways, simply by attending worship service together. I came to realize what an amazing group of people attend UCC. People shared so much of themselves in the safety of the small-group classes. I looked forward to my hour with adults and found the transition to the sanctuary with my children a much easier transition than I had thought. Eventually they didn't even sit with me and gathered with their youth group friends during the service (phew). Attending church on Sundays became a much better package with the addition of adult education.

As parents of young children, it feels as though we are striving 24/7 to make life better and more interesting for them. We do this with little to no time left for ourselves. The adult education model is a great way to offer one precious hour a week to hardworking adults. I am forever grateful for this concept and how it helped me become a better parent and person. It was a lifesaver for me as a single mother.

Debbie Wooten, mother, gynecologist, and former moderator at UCC Norwell

꒰ ꒱

WORSHIP FOR ALL

Of course, "Education for All" invariably meant we would be engaging in "Worship for All." The adjustment to having even our youngest children in worship proved to be more challenging than adding an extra hour to our Sunday morning experience. We tried our best to prepare for the transition in worship. We still provided nursery care for infants and toddlers, we made sure we had activity bags made up and set out for families with children who might struggle to pay attention, and we even offered Sunday morning classes for parents about how to parent in the pew. Even with those preparations in place, the children struggled, as did their parents. Our first month or two of worshiping together was undeniably noisy. Children were not used to worship, parents were not used to having them there, and it showed. However, we could not overlook the fact that for perhaps the first time in our history, we had an entire section of the sanctuary that was being frequented by teenagers who were now making worship a regular part of their lives. Interestingly, we also found that our older church members were the ones who were most enthusiastic about the inclusion of children in worship. These folks loved the fact that at least once a week they had the opportunity to be surrounded by youthful energy and excitement, and there was no question we had that in excess. We also realized that by having children with us in worship, we were breaking down an important barrier in our church. In previous years when we had church school during our worship hour, we had unwittingly prevented our youngest members from engaging in the full life of the church. The inclusion of our children in worship seemed like an important way of living out our open and affirming stance that strove to welcome all people into the full life of Christ's church. Thankfully, after several months, we noticed that children were becoming accustomed to being in worship for an hour. Our services became less noisy. And the children began to actively participate in the leadership of the service. Children now serve as acolytes, they receive the offering, some of our teenagers serve communion as deacons, and there are an increasing number of times when our young people lead worship with our pastors. On the rare occasion when we have an evening service where our youngest children are not present, their youthful energy and enthusiasm are keenly missed. While there are certainly issues that still exist in our current worship and educational model, most of our church leadership recognizes that it would be a huge loss to go back to the worship and educational model of the past. Learning together, worshiping together, and being together in fellowship are worth the challenges that come with just such a transition.

꽃 꽃

"Wow! Look at Karen's feet."

"Isn't she amazing?"

"Mommy, Daddy, how does she play the piano (organ) with her feet?"

"I don't know, she must be magic or she practices a lot! Shhhh!"

Today we still use similar tactics, but this was typical of many of our family interactions as we sat in our seats when we first arrived at UCC Norwell. Back then, we tried everything under the sun to get our kids to sit quietly and pay attention in church. We have even learned some new tactics along the way, like actually paying attention to the sermon. We can distinctly remember one of the first services we attended as a family. At that time we had been to church a few times so we bravely moved up to one of the front rows right in front of the choir. Little did we know that we had just found "our seats" for what has now been seven years. Then it was just the five of us: Kirsten, Charlie, Charlie (5), Kelsey (3) and Annalise (1)—curious Graham joined the crew three years later.

We can't recall much of the sermon that particular day. Chapin was certainly compelling and we were eager to hear his message, but our children had a different goal that day: DISTRACT EVERYONE WITHIN A TWENTY- FOOT RADIUS!!!

We remember feeling tremendous pressure to keep our kids quiet and under control as they giggled and climbed under and over seats. They were surely bothering everyone around us. We could feel everyone's eyes on us and we thought we knew what they were thinking— "Hey, could you keep your kids quiet?" At our wits end, we were ready to scoop them up and sneak out of the church. But when we looked across the way and saw a friendly face smiling at us with the unspoken message, "They're just being kids, don't worry about it!" We looked around and many people met us with the same smile and that "Don't worry about it" look. In the wake of this compassion and support from these strangers, we understood that we were in a unique and special place and that we and our children were certainly welcomed. We don't know if everyone enjoyed our children that day, but we were certain of one thing—we had found our church!

That first gift of compassion was just the beginning of a long list of gifts that we continue to receive from our UCC family. UCC Norwell is home to us. As church school teachers we have seen the growth in our kids and other children in the past seven years and look forward to many more years of faith journeys for our family.

> Charlie McNamara, fund-raiser and member of the Christian Education Ministry Team
>
> Kirsten McNamara, special education teacher and member of the Christian Education Ministry Team

꙳ ꙳

Objections Galore

It is important to note the particular challenges we faced during our time of transition, challenges and issues that still persist to this day. The issues and concerns that were voiced came almost exclusively from parents with young children. The issues were typically threefold. First, parents complained that doubling the time spent at church was too long a span of time for their children to manage. Second, some parents felt that having their children in worship with them didn't allow them to focus on the worship service—parenting in the pew tended to dampen adult enjoyment of the service. Finally, some parents lamented the fact that Sunday was the only day of the week their family didn't have to rush out of the house, and now the increased church commitment was doing just that.

While I felt personally grieved that church members were struggling with our new education model, their objections further fueled my belief that we were on the right track. It was interesting to note that parents felt their children were not able to be in the church building for two hours on Sunday when they expected their children to be able to handle two or three times that amount of educational time during the school week. As far as parents struggling in worship, I realized that parents had often viewed church school as nothing more than religious child care and did not want to be inconvenienced by having to play a central role in their children's education in worship. The objection to forcing our congregation to get up and get going even earlier on Sunday morning did initially strike a cord with me. Sunday was supposed to be the Sabbath, and perhaps our increased educational demands were stripping families of some of that sacred time. However, this objection fell flat when I learned that later that same year, the family with the most strenuous objections to our earlier schedule was now getting up at five o'clock every Sunday morning to take their children to hockey practice and games.

In the end, the most difficult aspect of our transition was the realization that education, worship, and fellowship within Christ's community are not priorities for everyone. Parents value secular education, and have higher expectations for their children in school, than they do for their children when it comes to faith education. For many families, organized sports are more important than organized religion. And many people refuse to take on much, if any responsibility at all, for the religious education of children. Some parents don't want to teach their children how to worship, and plenty of adults still refuse to teach church school. With the increased educational expectations of our church has come the increased realization that matters of faith often inhabit a rather peripheral location in our human and cultural landscape. This reality is certainly disappointing to those of us who make faith a priority, but it is helpful information when making decisions in the church. Now when we make a program decision in the church, we always try to determine what is best for the spiritual growth and development for our people, not what is easiest. The church's role is not to make life easier for people but to teach people how to live life better.

MARKERS OF SUCCESS

So, have we been successful? Yes and no. We have some wonderful success stories, to be sure. We have teenagers in worship. We have adults learning about their faith. We have children who feel included in almost every activity of the church. We have teachers who have the opportunity to both instruct and worship. We have senior citizens who thoroughly enjoy the youthful energy that swirls around them on Sunday mornings. We even have children who can now sit attentively through an entire service of worship. Another absolutely surprising marker of success was the increased financial giving we witnessed during the year of our educational transition. In a stewardship season when I suspected people would register their displeasure by decreasing their pledges, we saw one of the greatest increases in annual giving that has occurred in my ten years at UCC Norwell.

The failure we have witnessed is as singular as it is obvious. After five years, the vast majority of our church membership still does not engage in regular Christian education offerings. Plenty of families and individuals only attend worship. Therefore, the overall learning of the congregation remains modest. This is an issue we will continue to work on by trying to find new ways to attract people to the opportunities we have for them to learn about and further grow in their faith. "Education for All" and "Worship for All" is in some sense a daily battle we still engage in, and we have decided it is most certainly a hill worth dying on. In fact, if we want our people to understand themselves as ministers, they must first become disciples. Disciples are learners. In the Gospels, Jesus calls people to discipleship long before he sends them out two-by-two in ministry. If we are going to live out our Christian call to ministry, then we need to begin by becoming students of Jesus Christ. We believe ministry is the product of education; therefore education must be offered to everyone. We will feel successful when everyone in our congregation takes seriously their call to be a student of the Christian faith.

The Witness of Children

The true success of our education and worship model may be most clearly evidenced in the unprompted writings that have come from some of our younger children. Sitting in worship, one of our fourth graders decided to write her very own Prayer of Confession. We were so impressed by her efforts that we chose to use her prayer during the entire season of Lent. This is how Maggie McCloskey's prayer appeared in our worship bulletin:

> PRAYER OF CONFESSION (Written by a UCC Norwell 4th grader)
>
> Dear Lord, we are cruel and sinister at times, and we have not followed your ways with respect. Each glorious day that you bring us makes us wish we were free of our sins. Help us to learn the ways of Jesus Christ. Guide us to be compassionate of all people, and help us to see through their eyes. Fill our lives and souls with songs and prayer. Deliver us from evil and shine your light on us as we try to live in your ways. Hear our silent prayers, and please grant us your forgiveness...
>
> ASSURANCE OF PARDON
> Leader: God's love is greater than our sin.
> People: Jesus's compassion runs deeper than our failings.
> Leader: The Holy Spirit's mercy knows no limits.
> People: We have been forgiven. Alleluia. Amen.

Another child has taken copious sermon notes for the past several years, often drawing more meaning from the Scripture than the preacher on a given Sunday. What follows are a few of Jillian Williamson's worship and sermon reflections when she was in fourth and fifth grade.

November 23, 2008
Peace

Jesus is the king of peace. Two groups of people made peace—the Pilgrims and Indians. Years ago the Christians got together. When someone becomes ill, it is amazing because our church gives everything. I am fed in this community. We offer a healthy meal to everyone. We know so many people who share God's love.

March 1, 2009
Interrupted

Love your enemies. Eyes are open. Focus shifts every second. If God is real, why don't we see those signs? How hard is it for God to get our attention? There were two boats and Jesus put his foot on Peter's. Peter didn't like it. Peter does not want to go out again with Jesus but he says "yes, if you say so." Interruptions are plans to get our attention. Interruptions are holy invitations.

Palm Sunday 2010
Palms and Crosses

We don't like the cross. We wave palms in the air instead. When Jesus came on a donkey people were amazed and disappointed. Jesus didn't go to the thrown[sic] but went to teach. We wave palms in the air because Palm Sunday is happy for us. But Palm Sunday is not happy for Jesus. We need to turn our palms into crosses.

Our transition to a model of ministry that encourages education and worship for all is bearing good fruit. Seeds scattered in faith, as evidenced by the witnesses of our children, is proving to yield an important harvest.

We make plenty of mistakes, but every once in a while we are led to get things right, and worship and education for all has been one of the best steps our congregation has taken in the past ten years. It is a risk that continues to pay off in deeply meaningful ways. When we all take Christian Education seriously— when adults, youth, and children commit time to learning about Christian faith and discipleship—and when worship is an experience shared by each member of our community, our faith grows and faith witnesses abound. Our approach has been far from strategic, but we have been scattering seeds to the best of our ability, and we have experienced growth in unexpected and remarkable ways.

Questions for Reflection

1. What is your congregation's current practice regarding children in worship and educational offerings for adults?
2. If in your congregation, worship and church school for children are held at the same time:
   What are the known obstacles to including children in worship?
   What are the known obstacles to offering church school for adults?
3. Does your congregation have an education team with stated goals and objectives for learning among children, youth, and adults in the congregation? Do you use the language of discipleship when you talk about Christian education for all?
4. Does your worship team identify ways for children to participate in worship not only as worshipers but also worship leaders?

5. What is the congregation's degree of hospitality toward children in worship? For example, are they tolerant of occasional disruptions or do they expect noisy children to be removed promptly?

6. What is your experience of making changes in congregational practice during times of transition or crisis? If it's gone well, what helped make that possible? If it went poorly, what did you learn "for next time"?

PART 4

Harvesting

CHAPTER 9

Service to Others

A passion for mission and justice has always been at the heart of the United Church of Christ in Norwell. It is as if seeds of mission have been sown deep in the collective consciousness and spirit of our community, which results in a continual harvest of outreach initiatives that touch and change lives.

A HEART FOR SERVICE

In our church archives there is a black and white picture of a half dozen or so men standing in a field with shovels in their hands. Next to them is a hand-painted sign that reads, "Future Site of the United Church of Christ in Norwell." The field is unremarkable in most ways. It could be a grassy knoll or a rolling meadow any-where in the country, though the woolen trench coats bespeak a chilly climate for this upstart church to make its home. When I look at the photograph, I find myself wondering . . . could those folks have known what they were getting themselves into as they ceremonially wedged their spades into the earth at what was to become 460 Main Street in Norwell? Could they have dreamed that the foundation they were laying would support a community whose faith would touch the lives of countless people near and far? Could they have imagined that they were helping to birth a community that would fund and support dozens of other mission activities locally, nationally, and internationally?

Whenever I have asked that question of the charter members of our church, they all say they had no idea what would happen . . . they just wanted a church to call their own. However, those same charter members are quick to express their deep joy at the mission and outreach work that the congregation has engaged in over the years. For them to birth a church in Norwell that would affect rural health care in a place like El Salvador, or would help to build homes by organizing a local chapter of Habitat for Humanity, or would create a program of support for divorced, separated, and widowed people exceeded even their wildest hopes and dreams.

One of the marks of a truly vibrant Christian community is its involvement in missions to the poor. It is true that many mainline churches and denominations focus on mission, outreach, and social justice because those commitments are often easier to believe in than many of our Christian faith claims—we can all agree on the importance of feeding the hungry, while it is much more challenging to come to consensus on the resurrection of Jesus Christ. With that said, a focus on mission that arises out of Jesus Christ's call to tend to the needs of the poor can be the ultimate expression of love a community of faith can make to God's world. When faith and mission go hand in hand, it can be a powerfully life-transforming combination for all involved. The focus on mission at UCC Norwell stretches far beyond the hundreds of thousands of dollars committed to service organizations. Even though we are a relatively young congregation, the number of major mission initiatives that have been undertaken is quite remarkable. Mission seemed to grow organically in our church, with very little pastoral encouragement. Even when our church was struggling through the most difficult of relational challenges, the congregation's heart for service endured. As a result, unique opportunities for service have been pursued.

What follows are just a few of the life-transforming missions and ministries our community has engaged in. We offer our experiences as a witness to the kind of harvest that is possible when seeds of gospel hope are scattered with reckless and joyous abandon. Virtually all of these missions were lay-led efforts that were simply supported and encouraged by the pastoral leadership of our church. The mission work of our church has always sprung up directly from the people of our community.

New Nursery School

Back in the early 1970s, there was only one nursery school in the town of Norwell. The town was seeing an increase in families with infants and young children, and yet there were very few opportunities for early childhood education. UCC Norwell, which was only just getting its footing as a congregation, began to think it might be able to help meet a growing need in the community. In 1977, Jane Gammell, a member of our church, decided the town of Norwell needed a new nursery school, and she proposed starting just such a program in a single classroom in the basement of UCC Norwell. The young church enthusiastically supported the project, and the next academic year New Nursery School opened its doors to six students. In the years that have followed, New Nursery School has become a premier early childhood learning institution on the South Shore that accommodates hundreds of children from Norwell and our surrounding towns. New Nursery School also regularly extends scholarships for families in need so that everyone has the financial ability to have their children attend our school. New Nursery School has benefited our church in so many ways, but perhaps most importantly, it has introduced families who are new to our area to our church family. As is so often the case, a mission and ministry that was established to help the community outside our walls has served to enrich our church and draw in new members to our fellowship.

New Beginnings

In the early eighties, the church began to recognize that there was a population of people who were underserved, and historically maligned, by many churches. Divorced and separated people often feel isolated and abandoned by their family, their friends, and even the church. They are individuals who ache terribly, and they are often in desperate need of relational healing. So, in 1985, a couple of church members, with the support of pastoral leadership, crafted and launched a ministry to tend to the unique needs of divorced, separated, and widowed people. The ministry is called New Beginnings, and at its height, more than nine hundred people would come to our church for a time of small-group discussion, large-group programming, fellowship, and pastoral support on Monday evenings. The ministry was even initiated in a few other churches in Massachusetts. New Beginnings is a ministry we continue to run to this day. Every Monday night a few hundred members of New Beginnings gather to continue a powerful and essential ministry of support, encouragement, and healing. One of the most important roles the church of Jesus Christ can play in our culture and in the world is to identify communities that are discounted and discouraged and move to embrace them and help them toward healing and wholeness. We believe that is exactly what has happened, and continues to happen, each week at New Beginnings.

ASAPROSAR

One of the most life-transforming mission ministries in our church's history began more than twenty-five years ago when a member of our congregation, Eloise Clawson, accepted an invitation to visit El Salvador with a couple of our denominational leaders. The visit was made in the middle of the violent civil war in that country, which at the time was very much headline news in the United States. Despite the risks, a small delegation went to El Salvador to explore "The Role of the Church in Peacemaking." Vicky Guzmán, a doctor who was trying to bring health care to rural communities in her country, traveled with Eloise and the others serving as their guide. During the early years of the war, Dr. Guzmán had been imprisoned, because working with the poor was viewed as a communistic-subversive activity. Now she was ready to return to her work in the country, and the delegation traveled with her. Later, when the mission and outreach committee at UCC Norwell heard of the work in El Salvador, they sent the first $1,000 as seed money to enable Dr. Guzmán to again return to the country to continue her work.

A lasting relationship was formed between the United Church of Christ in Norwell and a new health organization called ASAPROSAR [Asociación Salvadoreña Pro-Salud Rural] (Salvadoran Association for Rural Health). Since 1985, our congregation has been making annual visits to Dr. Guzmán and ASAPROSAR, and Dr. Guzmán has made occasional visits to our congregation. The congregation got involved early on in supporting efforts to provide quality eye care to rural people. People living in poverty may wait years for an appointment for eye care and costs often prevent treatment. In a matter of months, a campaign to bring an annual eye clinic to El Salvador was under way. Since 1989, thousands of corrective eye surgeries have been performed, and tens of thousands of people have been fitted with eyeglasses. Each year our congregation continues to make two pilgrimages to our friends in El Salvador; in the summer a delegation is sent to spend time working with ASAPROSAR and the people they serve, and in the winter we help to send between fifty and sixty health-care professionals and other volunteers to El Salvador for the eye campaign.

This relationship has matured over the years and Dr. Guzmán reminds us that the concrete services cannot be underestimated but it is the relationships that endure. It is a culture that values relationships. "Come, work with the people we serve. Visit their homes, work with their children, share in their pride of family. You bring energy to our staff." We know without question that the relationship has been a rich blessing for our church community. As is most often the case with mission work, we find we have received much more than we have given from our sisters and brothers in El Salvador.

⚘ ⚘

Shortly before I left for El Salvador I began to wonder what I was really doing—visits to the doctor to get one vaccine after the next, trips to the pharmacy for anti-diarrhea medication, the most potent bug spray and handi-wipes for the latrines, and then leaving my four kids for a week. What was I thinking?!

Well, shortly after arriving back home from El Salvador I began to wonder what I was really doing back home and what this life is that I am leading. Why do I have this big house when families of six are living in shacks half the size of my bedroom? Do my kids really need several of the latest zip off pants and zip up shoes when children in El Salvador are thankful for one plain pair of each? And should I condone wastefulness when family members throw out plates of chicken because the sauce is sweet and sour, not barbecue, or toss a bowl of oatmeal that has too much cinnamon, or pour milk down the drain because it is warm when families in El Salvador would be grateful to have any plate of food?

The trip was an unbelievable experience for me. No newspaper or TV news flash could ever have prepared me for seeing poverty firsthand. We worked in the mountains of El Salvador among the sugarcane and corn and met families that are so poor. Their homes are small shacks nestled among the trees. Their floors are dirt and they have hammocks for beds. They are barefoot with little clothing, living on tortillas. We were also in the cities where there are guns and violence. Gangs are everywhere and the children are in danger and being abused. Many kids work with their parents in the market. They play in cardboard boxes behind their mother's produce cart from dawn until dusk and then slip into the back allies they call home. And everywhere around us there was trash. Trash upon more trash upon more trash. It litters the roads, the countryside, and their lives.

But, despite it all, the Salvadorans are warm and giving. Their eyes are bright and ASAPROSAR is giving them a future. The women are becoming educated, they're learning to run businesses and raise healthy families. They smile, shake your hand, and greet you with their eyes. They pray and thank God for a chance to better their lives. And through ASAPROSAR'S Barefoot Angels and Sprouts of Hope programs, the children are allowed to be kids. They are off the streets and have stopped scavenging for food at the dumps. They are safe and can run, sing, dance, laugh, and just play. They are happy, and they show you with one hug after the next. A beautiful little girl walked with me visiting homes in her village. We held hands for three hours. There is love in El Salvador. A young boy, Alex, gave me a bracelet off his wrist to remember him by and a woman gave me her chair at an outdoor meeting so I wouldn't have to stand in the rain. There is kindness in El Salvador. It was amazing to see the Salvadorans who have so little be so willing to give us what they have—simple gifts from their hearts.

So when I reflect upon the question, What is this life that I am leading—I now truly understand why Jesus said "Go, sell what you possess and give to the poor, and you will have treasure in heaven."

Leigh Williamson, mother, graphic designer, and member of Mission and Outreach team at UCC Norwell

꙳ ꙳

HABITAT FOR HUMANITY

One of the most widely recognized Christian mission and community service organizations in our country is Habitat for Humanity. Habitat for Humanity was founded in 1976 by Millard and Linda Fuller, who had a vision of eliminating substandard housing worldwide. Today, Habitat for Humanity has built more than 350,000 homes, sheltering more than 1.75 million people in more than 3,000 communities worldwide. As Habitat for Humanity was gaining notoriety in the early 1980s, a small group of our church members began to talk about starting a Habitat affiliate on the South Shore of Massachusetts. In 1985, South Shore Habitat for Humanity was established, with the organization making its home in our church building. Since its establishment, numerous church members have worked with, and for, the affiliate, and to date, South Shore Habitat for Humanity has built forty-nine homes in nineteen communities, helping to provide homes for more than eighty adults and one hundred and sixty children. Outside the United States, the South Shore affiliate has helped to fund and finance over one hundred and fifty homes in El Salvador, Peru, and Egypt. Our congregation's commitment to, and passion for, Habitat for Humanity's mission has taken us on numerous mission trips to work with affiliates in El Salvador; Slidell, Louisiana; Appalachia;

and other locations throughout the country. It continues to amaze me to think of how a handful of people with a mission and a vision can accomplish so much together. That echoes the truth of the Christian faith, which began with a teacher and a dozen disciples, and continues to transform the world for the good of all and for the glory of God.

Friendship Home

In 1999, a church member with a son with developmental disabilities began to have a vision for a community where developmentally disabled adults could gather together and establish lifelong friendships. The vision included multiple Friendship Clubs throughout the region where adults with developmental disabilities would gather for programs ranging from vocational training, life skills training, and fellowship. The ultimate dream was to have a fixed residence that would not only house Friendship Club gatherings, but would also serve as a respite facility so that families could get a break from the daily demands of tending to the needs of their developmentally disabled family members. Friendship Home was envisioned to allow families the ability to go to the grocery store, to doctor's appointments, or to have a weekend away. While all families with developmentally disabled children love their children and view them as great blessings, the need for a break from twenty-four-hour-a-day care-giving is essential to the overall health and well-being of the entire family. Friendship Home believes that times of respite help to enhance the care given within the families they serve. This need for respite care is not a need that our civic authorities recognize as a fundable priority, so for Friendship Home to become a reality, significant private funding needed to be raised. Ten years after the initial vision for Friendship Clubs and Friendship Home, we now have a gorgeous and expansive facility located toward the back of our church property. Friendship

Home has become a brick and mortar reality, and now we are blessed to have a thriving community of very special friends on our church property. Again, our call from Jesus Christ to reach out and serve people in need is wonderfully met by our partnership with Friendship Home. We believe that the church is responsible for tending to the very people our culture tends to forget. We are glad that friendship is a priority for the new community that now sits on the other side of our parking lot.

YOUTH SERVICE PROJECTS

In keeping with our church's commitment to mission, having our teenagers participate in service opportunities is a priority for our community. For the past few decades, our teenagers have spent their spring breaks from school together in service to others. These service projects have become the heart and soul of our youth ministry. When former members of our youth program look back on their experiences at our church, their most formative memories are the ones that came out of these service opportunities. Every spring a group of fifty to sixty teenagers and youth group leaders travel to work with people in need. They have served hungry and homeless people with Youth Service Opportunities Project in New York City and Washington, D.C. They have worked with Habitat for Humanity in West Virginia, Connecticut, and Pennsylvania. They have helped to build and maintain summer camp facilities for impoverished children in rural Georgia. One of the most moving service commitments our teenagers engage in during the year is the annual Holiday Ball, which they host for the South Shore Association for Retarded Citizens. Something of the presence of God is witnessed as formerly self-conscious teenagers shed their social discomforts and get out on the dance floor with developmentally disabled members of our South Shore community. Again, while we trust that these service opportunities are helpful and important to the people in need that are served, the real gift is to the teenagers themselves. It never ceases to amaze me how a self-centered and self-absorbed teenager can get on a bus for a week of service and return on that same bus a handful of days later a more thoughtful person. Parents are often the first to say that their children come back different, more generous, more respectful, and more grateful for the life they have been given. Beyond that gift, which is profound, is the blessed reality that many of the members of our youth program continue to engage in service to others while they are in college, and often wind up pursuing careers that they believe benefit the common good. The seeds of service, when sown in those who are young, wind up producing a heart for service that we hope lasts a lifetime.

Mission Tipping Point

As I run through all the many different hands-on service opportunities that our church engages in, I am a bit awed by the depth and breath of the commitments we keep—commitments that were not even part of the collective imagination of those church members who first dug shovels in the ground in a field where our church building now stands. The preceding list of mission activities is just a sampling of the ministry our church engages in. Every week you can find members of our community cooking meals for the Quincy Crisis Center, a faith-based outreach agency offering a 24-hour hotline, emergency food services, and advocacy programs; or for the Epiphany School, an independent, tuition-free middle school for children of economically disadvantaged families from Boston neighborhoods. Members of our church sort books for the Prison Book Ministry and sort food at the Boston Food Bank. We make room for numerous twelve-step programs in our building, and members of our church walk in support of many different causes. When I think of those ceremonial shovels turning

over the ground in a grassy meadow on a chilly day in late au-
tumn, I suspect "Build it and they will come" is not nearly as apt a
motto as "Do it and we will grow." As a community, we have grown
through service. Our teenagers have matured into more thoughtful and careful people because of their annual service projects that
connect them with people in need. Our adults have engaged in
life-tranforming relationships with our friends in El Salvador. Our
church's commitment to reach out beyond the walls of our church
to tend to the needs of our community has enlivened our imagination about how a midsize suburban church can effect change in
the world. We trust and pray that a commitment to mission and
justice will continue to be an area of growth for our church for the
rest of its life in this world.

I want to end on a note of deep humility and thankfulness. The
enthusiasm of this chapter is grounded in a general sense of awe in
regard to what the Holy Spirit has been able to accomplish within
our community. As a church, our experience of service to others
has felt more like a gift than an accomplishment. We would not
have been blessed to engage in the ministries we are involved in
if it had not been for the creative prompting and active sustaining
power of the Holy Spirit. In fact, if one were to look at a time line
of our church, they would certainly notice that most of our major
outreach initiatives were set in motion during the mid-1980s. That
was a time of great stability and goodwill within our congregation. As our church entered a time of division and strife in the
several years that followed, hardly any new mission initiatives of
lasting significance were pursued. Thankfully, mission commitments that had previously been established continued to maintain
momentum, but new ventures were not taken up. Perhaps some
of those deep mission commitments helped to sustain our community itself during those trying years of friction and infighting.
If there was ever a case to be made for the importance of church
unity and affection, it might be that a healthy and vibrant church
is able to look beyond itself to the needs of the world outside its

walls. With the advent in recent years of Friendship Home and Friendship Clubs, the Prison Book Ministry, and our relationship with the Epiphany School, I pray that we are in a time of stability and goodwill that will bear fruit in as dynamic ways as we have experienced in the past. Thankfully, what is at times impossible for us is always possible for the God we worship.

Questions for Reflection

1. Has your congregation experienced any time of internal strife when it was your outward focus, your active involvement in mission and outreach projects, that helped sustain your unity? What happened? What kept you together?

2. How do outreach and service opportunities come to the attention of your congregation? Does the pastor take the lead? Are individuals encouraged to pursue their passion? Are there committees or teams that shepherd projects? During worship, are needs and opportunities raised?

3. What is the mix of local, domestic, and international mission projects that your congregation supports? Do some of them offer "hands-on" projects for the congregation to participate in? How are children, youth, and adults involved?

4. How big can you dream when it comes to mission and outreach? What might your congregation begin, or what has your congregation begun, that could take on a life of its own as an independent organization?

CHAPTER 10

Evaluating Success with an Eye to the Future

UCC Norwell has been focused on cultivating vitality rather than strategizing about growth, because, we discovered, the spiritual growth of a congregation and of individuals is a mystery. God gives it, and usually in surprising ways. Yet, we have learned some things from our experience that I believe can inform our planning for the future and perhaps help other faith communities that want to scatter seeds and tend to the growth that God gives.

WHAT IS SUCCESS?

We have taken to writing down our story simply because so many churches have asked us to tell it. In many ways, we are a rather average and unremarkable church. We have our disagreements. We experience failure as often as we meet with success, and the successes we have had are quite different from the successes we were pursuing. We continue to grow numerically as a community, but not at the exponential rate that we hear about in the megachurch movement around the country. We make our home in a small town of which most people have never heard, and will never choose to visit. We still have Sundays when there are plenty of empty chairs in the sanctuary. As we write this book, I find myself wondering, what's the big deal? Our community has as many blemishes as the next church, what on earth do we have to teach anyone else? Sure, we have tried to scatter seeds of faith all around us, but much of it has not taken. Frankly, our practice of rather indiscriminatingly scattering seeds of mission and ministry all around us would never merit a business school case study, unless it were a story of the perils of disorganization. And yet, in our corner of spiritually chilly New England, there is an undeniable sense of life about our church. Regionally we are beating the odds, even if those odds are not the best markers of success. There are signs of progress.

A while back, wanting to somehow quantify, or at least identify, how much progress we had made as a Christian community, I asked a group of church members to spend some time reflecting on the meaning of a success as it relates to the life of Christ's church. Is success measured by increasing budgets and annual giving? Is success gauged in increased membership numbers and worship attendance? Is success about how many people like our church? If those are the markers of a successful Christian community, then we can pat ourselves on the backs and say, "Job well done." However, the group I assigned to the question of success came back to me with an answer that echoed the praise offered the wise servants in Jesus's parable of the talents as it is told in the gospel of Matthew. Success is standing before our Lord at the end of time and hearing Christ's words, "Well done, good and faithful servant . . . enter into the joy of your master" (Matt. 25:23, ESV). I am convinced that that is indeed the ultimate marker of success, for success is not something we judge for ourselves. Success can be judged by God alone, for only God knows the purpose for which we have been created. Only the creator is qualified to judge the accomplishments of creation.

When you were in the fifth grade, did you have a good idea of what success was? My vision of success in the fifth grade was to be the first baseman for the Boston Red Sox. My expectations did change over time, however, as I realized that success was more about understanding the special gifts and traits we all have and making the most of them wherever we may be planted.

I was shown what success is this last winter when I volunteered to help Chapin coach a fifth-grade basketball team, of which his son was a member. Although I had played much basketball when I was younger, I had never actually coached a team. Two fathers joined us in our efforts, so we usually had four adult coaches and eleven team members at our practices and games.

The record for the season was two wins and thirteen losses. A success. What? How can a two and thirteen season be a success? Is success measured exclusively by the score of a game or by a team's standing in the league? Is it measured by how many people attend the games? Is it measured by the color of the uniforms?

From the beginning, Coach Garner laid down two rules for success. The first was to hustle, the second was to have fun. Sounds easy. However, as the coaching seeds were being spread over the weeks of practices and games, I realized that other successes were also being met. Successes like having respect for yourself, your teammates, your coaches, the referees, and the other team. I watched seeds being scattered by instruction, stories, critiques, patience, and encouragement. I watched the boys give support to each other. I watched them improve their physical skills: shooting, dribbling, passing, rebounding, and coordination. I saw them learn that life is not always fair and that you do not quit. Basketball is a very fast sport and I observed them learning to look for opportunities as they appeared, and to take quick advantage of them.

On the last game of the season, a playoff game, it all came together for the boys. They played a team that matched up well.

Each one of the boys played as hard as they could. Not one of them let up. They dove for loose balls. They did what they had been taught. They supported one another. They showed courage. They made the coaches and their families and friends proud. They lost by two points. Big deal. They succeeded.

As these eleven boys look to their futures, some things are already obvious. Some will be leaders. Some will be questioners. Some will be salesmen. Some will be craftsmen. Some will be teachers. Some will be parents. Some will love the limelight and some will shy away from it. All will succeed if they cultivate the seeds that have been planted during this basketball season and throughout the other seasons of their lives. My hope is that they listen to their parents, their coaches, their teachers, their mentors, their bosses, their peers, and their subordinates, and through it all discern who they really are and build on those strengths and traits. And in the end, may it be said for each one of them, "Well done—good and faithful servant."

Jerry Thornell, financial administrator and gifts and call coordinator, UCC Norwell, and former financial manager, Polaroid Corporation

SIGNPOSTS: CHANGED LIVES

While it may be true that success can only be judged by God, that doesn't necessarily help us to know if we are making progress as a community of faith, particularly when progress is incremental. I do believe there are some sign posts for success that can be helpful in determining if we are advancing the gospel in our communities. First, I must object to the notion that some pastors and churches espouse when decline is experienced—that a church contracts in size because it is being more faithful than other churches. This seems to me to be a cop-out designed to make failing communities feel better about themselves. While there are occasions when important and prophetic decisions can lead to temporary attrition of church members, there is little if any biblical evidence that a shrinking faith community is a mark of success. In the Bible, increasing numbers of disciples and followers are an important sign that the Holy Spirit is blessing the teachings of a particular community. That said, the swelling crowds that followed Jesus and the first apostles were much more robust than the modest gatherings of disciples that Paul tended to draw together. While decline cannot be a marker of success, greater numbers of people drawn to the faith is not necessarily an indication of greater success among Christian ministries. I do not believe that a church that buys a former sports coliseum and fills it to capacity each Sunday is more successful than the small covenant community that lives out its faith by intentionally sharing a home in the center of a blighted urban neighborhood.

Since I am serving in a community that does not experience the kind of exponential growth worthy of national interest, I find I need to keep my eyes trained on the growing edges of our community to see if we are meeting with success. I look to signposts such as how many people gathered for Ash Wednesday service with an intention to observe Lent by engaging in a more rigorous set of spiritual disciplines. I look to stories of people who have given up addictions or obsessions because of the faith they encountered in our church. I look to summer worship attendance when the tug to stay away from church is all the more enticing. For me, success is found in the retired couple who finally gave up their eighty-eight-mile round-trip expedition to our church and decided to relocate so they could be close to our community. I don't know what words I will hear from Jesus at the end of time, but for now I gauge success by the increasing number of stories of lives changed because of the witness of our community.

Room for Growth

The truth of the matter is that the church of Jesus Christ will never be fully successful until the will of God is done on earth as we believe it is done in heaven. The ultimate success of the Gospel is the realization of a world where love abounds, justice prevails, and righteousness is at home. This means that we have a lot of work to do. If we are honest, love does not always abound, justice does not always prevail, and righteousness is not always at home in our churches, and that is true for UCC Norwell. When we look at our congregation, we recognize that there is plenty of room for growth within our community. We have mentioned numerous areas for growth in each chapter of this book. We have a "Church School for All Ages" which many members of our community resist participating in. We have a central mission as a church to encourage people to understand their whole life as ministry, and yet a relatively small portion of our community of faith wholeheartedly embraces that call. We have a church that could be both more *liberal* and *evangelical*. It is humbling to think that after all the work we have engaged in as a community, we still feel as though our ministries are just getting under way. Our ministry teams often need as much maintenance as our aging building does.

Perhaps there is a blessing in lacking a sense of accomplishment; it means that there are still plenty of adventures to be enjoyed, risks to be taken, and opportunities to be seized in our walk with Jesus. I suspect that a scattering seeds approach to church vitality, while somewhat unconventional, opens us up to the mystery of what the Holy Spirit of God might do with us next. In fact, if we ever feel as though we have truly "made it" as a congregation, that might be an indication that we have utterly failed. Christianity is not a monument to be admired but a movement to be advanced. The moment we stop planting is the time when the seasons of harvest have passed. For the church of Jesus Christ to be a vibrant and exciting place, there must always be room to grow—I thank God we have plenty of room at UCC Norwell!

PROJECT 2010

Ten years after launching Project 2000, in an effort to keep the Christian movement alive in our church in Norwell, we decided to take the opportunity to engage in a process of discernment for ourselves as a congregation. Desiring to gain a greater sense of where our congregation would be called to invest our gifts in the next ten years, we made an attempt to treat our entire church as if it were an individual going through our gifts and call discernment process. We called this process Project 2010, which may not have been an ideal name for a process we hoped would provide us vision for our life together as we approached the year 2020. Much of the project was structured to take place while I was away on sabbatical so that the church would have time to reflect on its own identity and call without my pastoral fingerprints all over the process.

Over several months, our church outlined its history—full of triumphs and bumps in the road. The community also studied cultural trends that might serve as challenges or opportunities for our congregation. Extensive surveying of our faith community was done so that the entire congregation had the opportunity to reflect on the gifts and calling of our church. When all the survey data was gathered, the church began to identify our particular gift set. After identifying our unique set of gifts as a church, the conversation shifted to areas where our congregation might invest our gifts in the world in the coming years. Over the course of this process we were glad to learn that people generally felt very positive about the health and overall direction of our church. That didn't mean that the process didn't effectively identify areas in our church life that required immediate attention. We were also glad to see that the historical commitments of our church still lined up well with where people perceived our gifts to be.

It was an affirming process, but upon my return from sabbatical, I couldn't help feeling as though it was not an entirely complete process. Something was missing—perhaps something central. I guess I had expected that upon my return I would be presented with ambitious new ministerial initiatives for us to launch into and enthusiastically pursue together. What I felt I received was a very thorough assessment of the health and vitality of our church, along with a fairly comprehensive list of areas in the life of our community that were in need of improvement. I began to wonder if we had missed the mark in the dreaming portion of our process. Maybe we were so focused on our life up until 2010 that we had forgotten to look to the horizon and the year 2020.

We began to plan a leadership retreat that would encourage people to dream about our future based on our current set of gifts as a community, and we are still engaged in this process now as I write. I hoped that together we would discover some new and daring faith adventures that would help to give focus and direction for our next decade together. After years of scattering seeds, perhaps now was the time to have a truly strategic vision and mission for our church. Maybe it was time to start planting in nice, neat, well-ordered rows! Thankfully, the Holy Spirit found a way to interrupt those plans and shift our focus to a daring venture that might fill our church with a fair amount of fear and trembling. It was time to start sharing our faith, our church, and our ministries with people outside our walls.

Getting Out of the Box

UCC Norwell is not particularly good at sharing the life of our community with people outside our church. Casual comments I've heard highlight one of our greatest and ongoing challenges as a congregation. One day I was waiting in line for a teller at a local bank when the husband of one of my church members saw me and warmly clapped me on the back, saying, "Chapin, my wife just raves about all the good work that you all are doing over at the UCC. She said that UCC is the best kept secret on the South Shore. If people knew what was going on there, the place would be a mob scene. Keep up the good work!" I remember another comment that a church member once made about homes. He said, "A house is just a box you live in." This statement reminded me that the church itself is a box, a box that can sometimes serve to inhibit our engagement with the people and communities outside our walls.

I am coming to the realization that the daring work we are called to over the next decade is to get ourselves out of our box at 460 Main Street in Norwell. Not only should we be *ministers* to the world, we should also begin to think about how we bring our *ministries* to the world. Whether we call it evangelism, or marketing, or simply sharing our faith, we don't do it well outside our church. We have so much to offer our community, and yet the only time we connect our ministries with people's lives is when they stumble into our community on a Sunday morning. There are risks when people go public with their faith, and those risks are likely ours to take in the years to come. The new adventure I sought for the congregation when I returned from sabbatical might simply be the old Christian venture of taking what we do and what we believe inside the church walls and sharing it with the world outside our walls for the sake of Jesus Christ and the glory of God.

A New England Witness

There are days when being a pastor, or a Christian, or a church in New England can be a bit disheartening. Faith is such a marginal commitment in our region. Many of us in the church fawn over the extravagant spectacles of Christian faith and followership we see taking root around the country. We see mega-churches and emergent church movements and high-profile preachers, and we wonder why that kind of ministry doesn't often take shape here. There are days when it can feel as though Christianity is faltering and failing in New England. And perhaps it is, and if that is the case it might be best for us to face up to that reality as soon as we can. If the death of the church in our region is what we fear, then we are forgetting the central claim of our faith that death is but a prelude to new and even more expansive life. Whatever cultural forces are working against Christ's church in a region like New England, those forces will eventually make their way around the country. We suspect that further diversity and plurality of belief, combined with the growing secularization of our society, will be challenges the church will have to face in the years to come. However, with challenges comes opportunity. Therefore, since the church in New England is now acutely experiencing some of those challenges, how we handle them can be very instructive to the movement of Christianity in our country for generations to come. Cultivating church vitality in a region like New England might hold the key to the future vitality of Christ's church in our nation. As difficult as it is to do and be church in New England, this might turn out to be a pivotal testing ground for the Christian church of the future. Our hope is that the work of our church can be a part of the exciting and ever-changing religious landscape of our country.

Keep Scattering Seeds

With such uncertainty before us, a strategic approach to ministry may be rather futile indeed. We don't know how the religious climate in our country will change in the coming years. We do not know if the environment will be hostile toward or welcoming of our faith efforts. We don't know what the spiritual soil of our region will be able to produce. We can try to plan for the future, but it is unlikely we will know how and where to dig our spades into the dirt. We do not know where growth might unexpectedly push up from the ground. Therefore, the vitality of our ministries and our churches might best be served by an extravagant sowing of seeds. We do not know what the future holds, but it is very possible that if we scatter the seeds of God's love and peace and justice so that not a single patch of ground is left uncovered, somewhere, somehow, beyond even our ability to imagine, the Holy Spirit will inspire a harvest of faith that increases thirty, sixty, one hundred-fold. The evidence for such a harvest seems modest at times, but there is a harvest to be had. It is happening in Norwell—it is happening in New England. And if vital ministry can be cultivated in New England, then vital communities of faith can take root anywhere—thanks be to God!

Questions for Reflection

1. What markers of success do you use, consciously and unconsciously, to evaluate your congregation's ministry? Are they helpful? Are they realistic? Are they grace-full?

2. Imagine Jesus at the end of time reviewing your congregation's mission and ministry and saying, "Well done, good and faithful servants." What do you see in your congregation now that would prompt such a response?

3. If your congregation were to take a scattering seeds approach to congregational vitality, how might you begin? Your responses to the "Questions for Reflection" in the previous chapters might give you some ideas.

Notes

Preface

1. "American Religious Identification Survey." Program on Public Values, Trinity College, 2009.

Chapter 4: A Vital Theology

1. In *Lost in the Middle?* (Herndon, VA: Alban Institute, 2009), Wesley Wildman and I discuss the fact that most "moderate Christians" have a mix of liberal and evangelical instincts but typically do not express themselves this way because of the polarized environment in which being both liberal and evangelical seems impossible. In fact, these moderates are routinely neglected in favor of the noisy extremes. They don't feel comfortable taking sides and can't see how victory by either side could possibly be a good outcome. When their church environment offers them one-sided rhetoric from the left or the right, some counter by finding creative ways to nurture their own spirituality. Others leave churches altogether in search of a more faithful and integrated religious life. Most stay where they are, with their frustration and longing as constant reminders that something is wrong and that there must be a better way. Our first book is a resource that

will help moderate Christians articulate their personal faith and their congregational identities. It will inspire them to work for Christian unity in the face of the seemingly intractable war between the polarized opposites of secularized liberalism and conservative evangelicalism.

Found in the Middle! (Herndon, VA: Alban Institute, 2009), our second volume, describes churches made up of moderate Christians who have found each other and aim to model for the world a kind of community that rises above territorial instincts and insults, one that stresses love and acceptance more than cultural identity and security. Some say it is enough if people worship together. Based on our own experience and drawing on considerable research into congregations, we disagree. Worship functions as vital glue for keeping moderate Christians together in the face of the stresses of disagreement. But the preached message matters just as much. If sermons and education do not help people talk confidently about their faith to each other and to those beyond the borders of their community, then worshipful togetherness will never survive the ordinary trials of disagreement. If an intentional community cannot have a vision of Christian good news in common, then their corporate faith risks becoming a formless muddle briefly masquerading as joyful pluralism.

Chapter 6: The Ministry of the Laity

1. Center for Dependable Strengths, www.dependablestrengths. org.
2. Luther Seminary, St. Paul, MN, www.centeredlife.org.